THE COMPLETE ILLUSTRATED
KITCHEN DOCTOR
BOOK OF HEALING RECIPES

THE COMPLETE ILLUSTRATED

KITCHEN DOCTOR

BOOK OF HEALING RECIPES

**THE RIGHT FOODS FOR HEALTH, THE RIGHT DIET FOR
YOUR BODY, THE RIGHT RECIPES FOR YOUR LIFESTYLE**

Editor
Jill Scott

HERMES
HOUSE

This edition published by Hermes House

Hermes House is an imprint of
Anness Publishing Limited
Hermes House
88–89 Blackfriars Road
London SE1 8HA

Tel: 020 7401 2077
Fax: 020 7633 9499
www.hermeshouse.com; www.annesspublishing.com

If you like the images in this book and would like to investigate using them for
publishing, promotions or advertising, please visit our website
www.practicalpictures.com for more information.

© Anness Publishing Limited 2000, 2006

A CIP catalogue record for this book is available from the British Library.

Publisher: Joanna Lorenz
Executive Editor: Linda Fraser
Project Editor: Susannah Blake
Designer: Ian Sandom
Reader: Kate Humby
Production Controller: Lee Sargent
Photographers: Karl Adamson, Edward Allwright, Steve Baxter, Nicki Dowey, James Duncan, Ian Garlick, Michelle Garrett, Amanda Heywood, Janine
Hosegood, Dave Jordan, Dave King, Don Last, William Lingwood, Patrick McLeavey, Michael Michaels, Tom Odulate, Peter Reilly, Sam Stowell
Recipes: Catherine Atkinson, Angela Boggiano, Carla Capalbo, Jacqueline Clarke, Carole Clements, Kit Chan, Trish Davies, Roz Denny,
Nicola Diggins, Matthew Drennan, Sarah Edmonds, Joanna Farrow, Christine France, Silvana Franco, Shirley Gill, Carole Handslip, Christine Ingram,
Manisha Kanani, Lesley Mackley, Norma Macmillan, Sue Maggs, Kathy Mann, Norma Miller, Sallie Morris, Annie Nichols, Maggie Pannell,
Jennie Shapter, Anne Sheasby, Laura Washburn, Stephen Wheeler, Kate Whiteman, Elizabeth Wolf-Cohen, Jeni Wright

Previously published as Healing Foods for Special Diets

1 3 5 7 9 10 8 6 4 2

NOTES

For all recipes, quantities are given in both metric and imperial measures and, where
appropriate, measures are also given in standard cups and spoons. Follow one set of
measures, but not a mixture, because they are not interchangeable.

Australian standard tablespoons are 20ml. Australian readers should use 3 tsp in place
of 1 tbsp for measuring small quantities of gelatine, flour, salt, etc.

American pints are 16fl oz/2 cups. American readers should use 20fl oz/2.5 cups in
place of 1 pint when measuring liquids.

Electric oven temperatures in this book are for conventional ovens. When using a fan
oven, the temperature will probably need to be reduced by about 10–20°C/20–40°F.
Since ovens vary, you should check with your manufacturer's instruction book
for guidance.

Medium (US large) eggs are used unless otherwise stated.

Soy sauce contains wheat flour and is unsuitable for wheat- or gluten-free diets. As
a substitute, use tamari, which is also made from soya beans but is rice based. It is
readily available from health stores.

Many commercial stock cubes contain MSG (monosodium glutamate), which can be
made from wheat starch, and are therefore unsuitable for wheat- or gluten-free diets. If
there is no time to make your own stock, look for bouillon cubes or powders that are
labelled "gluten-free" or use chilled stocks, which are available from larger supermarkets. Always read the ingredients list on any food product to check that it is "safe"
to eat for any special diet.

ALLERGY-FREE RECIPES
The recipes in this book have an at-a-glance guide to the foods
that each is free from:

 Gluten-free

 Wheat-free

 Corn-free

 Dairy-free

 Nut-free

 Fish and Shellfish-free

 Egg-free

Yeast-free

Soya-free

CONTENTS

PREFACE

The way we live our lives today, in a fast-moving world of technology, means we often have less time to look after ourselves properly. Most people are less active than they should be. They eat diets that are too high in fat and too low in fruit and vegetables, and live busy and stressful lives. As a consequence, there is a greater risk of heart disease and other serious illnesses, as well as weight problems and even obesity. But the good news is that we can do something about it.

Choosing to follow a healthy lifestyle can help you to live longer and make the most of your life. The main focus of this book is on the dietary aspects involved, but to attain the real benefits, it is important to look carefully at your life as a whole.

Working towards leading a healthier lifestyle means not only eating well but also being more physically active, not smoking and taking "time out" for relaxation. You can have the healthiest diet possible, but the benefits will be reduced if you smoke cigarettes or rarely take exercise.

Even apparently small changes in your daily lifestyle can make a noticeable difference to your overall health and help to improve your energy levels and general quality of life.

THE BENEFITS OF A HEALTHY LIFESTYLE

Taking care of yourself by trying to change your habits and live more healthily will help you to:
• Gain confidence in how you look and feel.
• Manage your weight better.
• Lower your risk of developing serious illnesses such as heart disease, high blood pressure, diabetes, obesity and some forms of cancer.
• Achieve a positive outlook and feeling of well-being.

LIFESTYLE GUIDELINES

Scientists and nutrition experts recommend the following five key guidelines for a healthy lifestyle:
• Be active in your daily life.
• Make sure your leisure time is varied and stimulating.
• Aim for five or more servings of fruit and vegetables a day.

• Base meals around starchy foods, such as rice and pasta.
• Choose low-fat or lower-fat foods whenever possible.

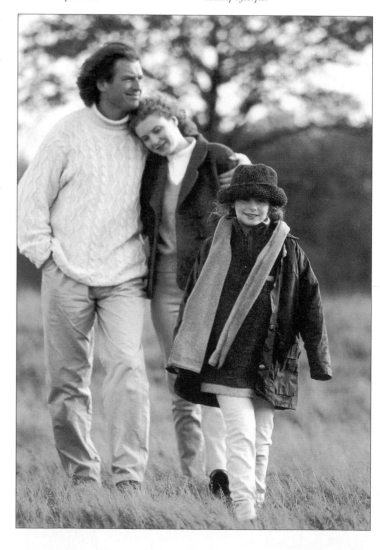

Below: Enjoying active leisure time, such as a walk in the countryside or in a city park, can help you on your way to achieving a healthy lifestyle.

THE LINK BETWEEN DIET AND HEALTH

There is no doubt that what we eat affects our health, and there are now proven links between diet and disease. Diseases that are known to be linked to diet include heart disease, osteoporosis, cancer, diverticular disease, constipation and other digestive disorders.

OBESITY

Throughout the developed world, evidence suggests that the number of people who are overweight or obese continues to rise. Both dietary factors and physical inactivity are linked to the development of obesity. Being overweight can be detrimental to good health and is associated with an increase in cardiovascular disease risk factors, such as high blood pressure (hypertension), high blood cholesterol levels and diabetes. Being overweight and obese can also aggravate other existing problems that are otherwise unrelated, such as osteoarthritis.

Scientists agree that dietary change is essential if we are to see a reduction in the prevalence of heart disease, strokes and certain types of cancer. Recommendations have been made about specific dietary changes, in particular the reduction of fat, especially saturated fat. Many people consume more than the recommended daily intake of fat, which should be no more than 35 per cent of dietary energy, and most people would benefit from switching to lower-fat options.

Right: Foods that are high in saturated fats can increase your risk of heart disease.

CARDIOVASCULAR DISEASE

A diet high in saturated fat is known to be one of several risk factors in the development of cardiovascular disease, which includes heart disease and strokes, and which accounts for a huge number of deaths every year. Nutrients such as those contained in fish oils, the anti-oxidants found in fruit and vegetables, and possibly dietary fibre, are all believed to help in protecting against the development of heart disease.

CANCER

It is estimated that, worldwide, some 7.6 million people will develop cancer and 5 million will die of the disease every year. Diet is believed to be linked to 10–70 per cent of all cancers. This compares with estimates of 30 per cent for smoking, 3 per cent for alcohol, about 4 per cent for occupation and 10 per cent for infections. Dietary factors are particularly associated with colo-rectal cancer, stomach cancer, and possibly oral and oesophageal cancer.

Left: Foods such as oily fish, fruit and vegetables are believed to protect against many diseases, such as cancer.

HEALING FOODS AND SPECIAL DIETS

We all need food for life. It provides us with the nutrients we need to stay healthy. Some foods are healthier than others, and can help to lower our risk of developing certain diseases, such as some cancers and other degenerative disorders.

Fresh fruit and vegetables, for example, are packed with health-giving nutrients, such as antioxidants, flavenoids and phytochemicals, as well as many other important constituents, which can have a protective effect on our health.

Sometimes, changes to the diet are needed to treat or manage a diagnosed condition, such as a food allergy or diabetes. In other words, it may be necessary to follow a special diet in which the healthy eating guidelines are adapted to suit individual needs.

Whatever your condition or food sensitivity, it is vital that your diet continues to provide the essential nutrients that your body needs. Careful substitution of one food or group of foods can be achieved with a little thought and planning. For example, if milk and dairy foods are excluded from the diet, it is essential that you continue to include foods that will provide sufficient calcium, because dairy foods are the richest dietary source of calcium.

Thankfully there is now a good range of alternatives to dairy foods, mainly in the form of soya, such as soya milk and soya desserts, so it can be quite easy to substitute one product for another. Try to opt for the calcium-fortified varieties, because soya is not naturally a good source of calcium. This will help to boost your daily calcium intake. The section on cow's milk intolerance offers more practical advice about which foods can be included in the diet to ensure a healthy calcium intake.

The more restricted a diet is, the more difficult it will be to meet all of your body's nutritional requirements. This is because variety is the key to a healthy, balanced diet and eating a variety of different foods every day is the easiest way of ensuring a healthy diet. If the variety of foods that you can eat is restricted, particularly if several different groups of food are avoided, more care is needed when planning your diet. If you find this very difficult, then a dietary supplement may be needed to boost your intake of essential vitamins and minerals.

There might be other reasons why someone decides to change his or her diet. The healthy eating guidelines outlined in each section form the foundation of a well-balanced diet, but you may choose to fine tune these to suit your own needs, or to include foods that you believe will reduce your risk of developing other diseases, such as cancer or heart disease.

There is certainly good scientific evidence that the antioxidant nutrients, particularly vitamin A, in the form of betacarotene, vitamin C and vitamin E, can help prevent the build up of

Left: A diet that is rich in fruit and vegetables is essential for good health. Aim to eat five or more portions of fruit and vegetables a day.

compounds called free radicals, which are thought to be responsible for triggering cellular damage, resulting in the development of serious illness.

Betacarotene and vitamin C in particular are associated with protection against the development of certain cancers. Good sources of betacarotene include yellow or orange fruits and vegetables, such as carrots, tomatoes, pumpkin, red peppers, apricots and peaches, as well as green leafy vegetables, such as broccoli and spinach. Rich supplies of vitamin C can be found in citrus fruits and juices, kiwi fruit, blackcurrants, strawberries and tomatoes.

Vitamin E is associated with protection against heart disease. Good food sources of vitamin E include vegetable oils, particularly sunflower oil; almonds; wholegrain breakfast cereals and bread; eggs; avocados; dairy products; margarines and spreads.

One of the best ways of increasing your intake of these valuable health-giving nutrients is to eat five or more portions of fruit and vegetables each day. In parts of the world where people eat lots of fresh fruit and vegetables, such as Mediterranean countries, the incidence of both heart disease and cancers is much lower.

Above: Eating can be one of the greatest pleasures in life, so take time out to enjoy meals in a calm and relaxing environment with your friends and family.

THE PLEASURES OF EATING

In all the discussions around what to eat and what to watch out for, it is important not to forget that eating is also a very enjoyable everyday activity. It is important that food is eaten not just for health but also for taste, and – sometimes – for pure indulgence. Even on a very restricted diet, try not to cut out all of your favourite foods, and enjoy them occasionally as a treat.

ALLERGY-FREE EATING

If you have ever developed a bad migraine or an irritating skin rash,

it may be that the condition was caused not by illness but by

something to which you are allergic or sensitive. The idea of changing

your eating habits and cutting out certain foods that you are used to

eating may seem like a daunting task. This chapter provides all the

practical advice you will need, from recognizing an allergic reaction

to isolating the culprit and maintaining a healthy diet.

INTRODUCTION

Allergic reactions, intolerances and sensitivities can take many different forms, and can prove difficult to pinpoint. Although they are not thought of as illnesses, they can sometimes make the sufferer feel extremely unwell, as anyone with asthma or hayfever will tell you. Depending on the nature and severity of your symptoms, the problem can be either a mild, short-term nuisance or a more serious, long-term condition, such as asthma or coeliac disease.

The potential causes of an allergic reaction are numerous and can be difficult to identify. The aim of this chapter is to help you discover if something that you are eating or drinking could be the cause of your symptoms. Once you've tracked down the cause, this chapter has helpful advice on how to adapt your diet to be nutritionally balanced while excluding anything to which you're sensitive. By investigating your symptoms and excluding suspect foods from your diet, you can discover those responsible for the reaction and use the delicious and easily prepared recipes in the second part of the book to help you enjoy a healthy, allergy-free life.

CAUSES AND REACTIONS

An allergy is a reaction that occurs when the body's immune (defence) system overreacts to a normally harmless substance, causing irritation, disability and sometimes even fatality. A substance that causes an allergy is called an allergen and can be anything in the environment – whether it's something ingested, inhaled or that touches the skin – that causes an adverse reaction. Among the most commonly found allergens are pollen, house-dust mites, pet hair, insect stings, chemicals or food and drink.

Our immune system usually protects us from harmful foreign invaders, such as viruses and bacteria, that might otherwise cause illness. In the allergic person, however, the system believes that the allergen is damaging and reacts to it accordingly. A special type of anti-body, called IgE (immunoglobulin E), is produced to fend off the threatening substance. This in turn leads the special "mast" cells in our bodies to release further chemicals, the best known being histamine, which join the IgE antibodies in attacking the invading material. The result is an allergic reaction, with its associated symptoms. The site of the reaction will depend on where the mast cells are located, and is often in such places as the nose, skin, lungs or intestines. Typical allergic reactions and their symptoms include vomiting and diarrhoea; hayfever; asthma (coughing, wheezing and breathlessness); perennial rhinitis (blocked or runny nose); urticaria or hives (skin rash); and eczema (mild to severe dry skin condition).

Below: Pet hair may cause an allergic reaction that results in irritation to the eyes, nose and skin, and difficulty in breathing.

HOW COMMON ARE ALLERGIES?

It is not known just how common allergies are because the potential causes are numerous and can be difficult to identify. It is not even known exactly how many people react badly to certain substances, since many cases are mild enough to be undetected or may be misdiagnosed.

Allergies (particularly asthma and hayfever) appear to be on the increase and this may be a consequence of aspects of contemporary living, such as increased air pollution and more use of chemicals and pesticides.

It has also been suggested that because modern medicine has reduced our risk of infection from "naturally" harmful foreign invaders, such as bacteria, our immune systems are now insufficiently challenged, leading to a reaction, in genetically susceptible people, to ordinarily harmless substances. Greater awareness and recognition of allergies may also be a factor in our perception of the problem: it is important not to use the term indiscriminately as a convenient scapegoat for all kinds of ailments and complaints that have never been proved to be the result of an allergic reaction.

Surprisingly, the onset of an allergy or intolerance can occur at any age and the substance causing it may be something that has previously been tolerated. Equally, sensitivity can be outgrown, and troublesome symptoms can completely disappear.

SUSCEPTIBILITY TO ALLERGIC DISEASE

There is a strong genetic link with the development of allergies. If someone in your family – a parent, for example – has an allergy to something, it is quite likely that this susceptibility may be passed on. It is also thought that some people have a susceptible immune system, particularly if they have increased levels of the IgE antibody (immunoglobulin E). Children with

Above: Eggs, citrus fruits, peanuts and shellfish pose a problem for many people.

high levels of blood IgE often suffer from asthma and hayfever, and may also be allergic to some foods.

THE DIFFERENCE BETWEEN ALLERGY, INTOLERANCE AND SENSITIVITY

Strictly speaking, the word "allergy" should only be used to describe a specific response caused by an over-reaction of the immune system. An intolerance, however, is a broader term describing any unpleasant reaction to an offending substance. Hyper-sensitivity can be used as a general description covering both allergy and intolerance, although none of these should be confused with food aversion, which has psychological roots.

There are many different causes of food intolerance, which may be linked to the behaviour of various enzymes or bacteria in the body. Lactose (milk sugar) intolerance, for example, is not an allergic reaction but occurs because a person has insufficient lactase

enzyme, which is needed for the digestion of lactose.

There are also a number of substances in food that can cause a reaction in some people. Caffeine in tea, coffee, chocolate and cola, for instance, can bring on palpitations and restless behaviour, while amines found in red wine, chocolate and cheese can trigger a migraine. These are not true allergic reactions, although the term is frequently used loosely for describing all sorts of food intolerance.

NON-FOOD ALLERGENS

Discover the cause of your allergy, then take action to avoid the substance or to minimize your exposure to it. Could one of these allergens be to blame?
House-dust mites Modern homes often have fitted carpets, double glazing, central heating and poor ventilation, providing ideal conditions

for house mites to thrive. You should vacuum regularly, wet-wipe surfaces, consider wood, lino or other hard flooring rather than carpets, and blinds rather than curtains. Open windows as often as possible.

Bee and Wasp Stings These may cause pain and swelling and can even occasionally cause anaphylactic shock.

Jewellery Metal allergy (especially to nickel) can cause skin irritation.

Medicines Aspirin and penicillin and other antibiotics can cause an allergic rash. Aspirin may cause asthma.

Pets Both fur and feathers can be responsible for allergic rhinitis, asthma and eczema.

Pollen Hayfever is a very common allergy. It causes itchy eyes, sneezing and a blocked nose, especially when the sufferer ventures outdoors, and particularly in early summer. To reduce the symptoms, it is best to avoid over-exposure by closing windows and wearing sunglasses.

Toiletries and Cosmetics Some perfumed products can be a problem so try changing to a pure formulation or using non-allergenic make-up.

Above: Beauty preparations and soaps with non-allergenic formulae are now widely available and popular for their purity.

COMMON ALLERGIES AND THEIR SYMPTOMS

Allergic Disease	Allergen	Typical Symptoms
Hayfever (seasonal)	Pollen	Sneezing, streaming eyes, blocked nose
Asthma	Dust mites, animal hair, pollen	Coughing, wheezing, breathlessness
Allergic Rhinitis (perennial)	Dust mites, animal hair	Sneezing, runny nose, itchy eyes
Urticaria (skin rash)	Food, medicines	Itchy rash, characterized by the eruption of weals or "hives"

FOOD ALLERGIES

Allergic Disease	Allergen	Typical Symptoms
Coeliac Disease	Gluten (protein found in wheat, barley, rye and oats)	Poor growth, weight loss through vomiting and diarrhoea, tiredness
Peanut Allergy	Peanuts (and possibly other nuts and seeds)	Can cause a massive, potentially fatal reaction called anaphylactic shock, where the victim finds it hard to breathe, turns blue around the lips and faints or loses consciousness
Wheat Allergy	Wheat and wheat products	Asthma, itchy skin, diarrhoea
Egg Allergy	Eggs and egg products	Eczema or urticaria
Fish Allergy	Fish and shellfish	Urticaria in mild cases, but can lead to anaphylactic shock in severe cases
Milk Allergy	Milk protein	Eczema, asthma, perennial rhinitis, intestinal upsets

A small minority of people may also be allergic to food additives, both natural and artificial, such as food colours like tartrazine and anatto and preservatives such as benzoate. However, as the chart shows, symptoms are often similar for different allergens, so it is essential to pinpoint the true cause.

TRACKING DOWN THE PROBLEM

The first step in investigating any potential food allergy or intolerance is to speak to your family doctor, who should initially make sure that your symptoms are not due to any other illness. He or she will try to diagnose the problem by asking questions about your diet and lifestyle and whether you've noticed if symptoms are worse at any particular time. The medical profession varies in its attitude and approach to the treatment of allergies. You may be referred to a special hospital unit or clinic for further investigation or you could be advised to see a dietician, if dietary changes are to be considered. Many clinics offer allergy testing by a variety of methods, which are described below. While these may prove useful, not all of these methods are recognized by the medical profession as providing reliable results.

IS AN ALLERGIC REACTION LIKELY TO BE IMMEDIATE?

In cases of severe, acute allergy (which susceptible individuals may experience after eating peanuts, fish, eggs or sesame seeds) reaction is immediate and can be life threatening. After a first attack, those affected will be well aware of their allergy. It is vital that they avoid the offending food and always carry appropriate treatment, such as steroid inhalers, antihistamine tablets or emergency adrenaline (for anaphylaxis/anaphylactic shock).

Acute reactions to milk (and wheat) tend to be less severe and are often delayed (12–48 hours after ingesting the trigger food). In infants, severe acute reaction can occur, but as the diet is limited, the offending trigger is usually obvious – as when formula milk is introduced after breastfeeding. Recurring headaches, skin complaints, sinus or digestive problems are likely to be caused by something environmental or something eaten regularly, which is why milk or wheat is often suspected.

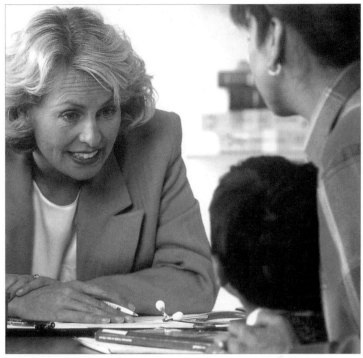

WHAT METHODS ARE USED TO TEST FOR ALLERGIES OR INTOLERANCES?

The RAST (Radio Allergo Sorbent Test) This test can be used for identifying acute allergies when there is an immediate reaction, by measuring IgE (immunoglobulin E) antibody levels in the blood.

The Skin Prick Test A few drops of the suspect allergen (prepared to a standardized concentration) are put on the skin, which is then pricked, so that the allergen seeps underneath. After a brief delay, the allergist looks for signs of a reaction. The test is quite successful for detecting environmental allergies, such as pollen or cat hair, which exhibit immediate sensitivity, but may be less useful for food intolerances, which are often delayed. However, extreme allergic disorders, such as anaphylaxis, do usually give a positive skin prick test.

Above: If you suspect that you or someone in your family may be suffering from an allergy, the first thing to do is make an appointment with your doctor.

The Vega Test In this test, an electrode is placed on an acupuncture point or held in the hand. It is said to detect whether a substance placed on the machine causes you to react, but again tests may not be reliable.

Lactose intolerance in infants may be diagnosed by checking stools for acidity (lactic acid is a by-product of undigested lactose).

Exclusion and Challenge Diets These provide the most accurate and effective means of discovering a food intolerance. The sufferer excludes suspect foods, waits to see whether there is an improvement in symptoms, then gradually reintroduces them. For more information, see "Testing for Food Allergies".

TESTING FOR FOOD ALLERGIES

Diet investigation is often used to try and discover the cause of food sensitivities. Depending on which food(s) are suspected, the diet may be relatively simple or involve the dieter in a substantial amount of thought and commitment.

In cases of multiple food intolerance, it is far more difficult to discover the whole problem and, because psychological factors may influence a person's perception of how a food affects them, blind testing may be advised so that an accurate diagnosis can be obtained.

Food intolerances are often not lifelong sensitivities. People find that after a rest period the offending food can be reintroduced gradually. However, the food should only be eaten infrequently; eating too much or too often may trigger a repeat of the previous symptoms.

Different clinics and specialists will vary in their approach towards dietary testing, so follow the advice given by your own dietician. Whatever the diet, it is essential that you stick to it rigidly as any lapses will affect the validity of your results.

SIMPLE EXCLUSION DIET

If you have a fairly good idea about which single food is causing you a problem, it is a simple matter to exclude it from your diet and see if the symptoms disappear or improve. It is quite easy to avoid some foods, such as cheese, red wine and citrus fruits, but if a major food group, such as dairy products or wheat is suspected, you will need to take professional advice from a dietician on how to modify your diet safely without missing out on important nutrients. After avoiding the suspect food for a few weeks, try eating

Below: Common trigger foods that cause food intolerances and allergies include dairy products such as milk and yogurt, wheat, nuts, citrus fruits and citrus drinks, coffee, chocolate, eggs and shellfish.

it again and see if the symptoms return. If you have experienced a severe allergic reaction to a particular food, such as peanuts, don't attempt to try the food again. You already know the cause of the problem and are strongly advised not to risk repeating the reaction.

ELIMINATION DIET TIPS AND GUIDELINES

• Don't choose a busy time, whether at work or at home, to undertake an elimination diet; you need to be stress-free.
• Prepare and plan ahead, so that you don't run out of suitable foods and can easily cater for other members of the family.
• Do not skip meals.
• Try to base your diet on fresh foods as much as possible.
• Stick to plain cooked dishes because using a lot of ingredients in recipes will make detection all the more difficult.
• Avoid eating out, or if you do, choose plainly cooked dishes.
• Make a note of the ingredients used in any manufactured foods.
• Plan some non-food treats for yourself, such as a trip to the hairdresser, a manicure or a sauna, so that you don't focus all your attention on your diet.

MULTIPLE FOOD EXCLUSION DIET

If it's suspected that there is a dietary cause for your symptoms but the offending food is not known, it may be suggested that you cut out common trigger foods, which are known to cause problems most frequently. These foods include milk and dairy products, eggs, shellfish, wheat, citrus fruits, nuts, coffee, chocolate and azo dyes, and also possibly corn, yeast and soya.

You will need to follow this diet for two to three weeks to see if any improvement occurs. If symptoms ease or disappear, the excluded foods should

Below: A strict elimination diet permits only foods that rarely cause allergy problems, such as lamb, turkey, rice, potatoes, broccoli, cauliflower and pears.

then be reintroduced individually, allowing an interval of several days between each. If the symptoms reappear, you have your answer – although several repeat exercises may be necessary to be sure of the diagnosis.

If there is no improvement while following the diet, either some other food could be responsible (and you may be advised to try the simple exclusion diet) or you will need to investigate other, non-dietary causes.

STRICT ELIMINATION DIET

This very strict diet consists of only a few basic foods that are rarely known to cause a reaction. Because it severely limits the food selection, a strict elimination diet is only advised in extreme cases where medication does not provide any relief. Foods that are commonly allowed include lamb or turkey, potatoes, rice, pears, cauliflower or broccoli (and sometimes other vegetables), sunflower or olive oil and bottled water. The exact range of permitted foods may vary at the discretion of your consultant.

The diet is followed strictly for two to three weeks. Foods are reintroduced one by one, and any change of symptoms observed.

RARE FOODS DIET

This is basically the same as the strict elimination diet, except that some more unusual foods, such as exotic fruits and unusual vegetables and meats, are allowed. The theory behind this diet is that people are less likely to react to foods that they have not eaten (or rarely eaten) before. If symptoms still persist on this diet, then the likely diagnosis is that the person is not food-sensitive and that some other factor is responsible, or that the person has an undiagnosed medical condition.

FASTING

This is a drastic measure that is not generally advised because of the risk of severe nutritional disorders that may

---

FOOD DIARY

Date : *Monday 24th*

Meal	Food / Drink	Time taken	Symptoms
Breakfast	*orange juice* *2 slices of toast* *spread with butter* *& marmalade* *cup of tea*	*7.45am*	
Mid-morning	*cup of coffee* *chocolate biscuit*	*10.30am*	
Lunch	*cheese sandwich* *packet of crisps* *strawberry yogurt*	*12.30pm*	*Migraine about 2.00pm*
Mid-afternoon	*cup of tea* *jam doughnut*	*3.00pm*	
Evening meal	*grilled fish* *new potatoes and peas* *glass of white wine*	*7.00pm*	

Additional Notes
Difficult day at work – felt very stressed and tired.
Might be starting a cold, sneezing a lot and felt rather blocked up.

---

affect the balance of your health. It is not advisable to attempt such an extreme regime, whether for intolerance testing, weight loss or any other dietary reason.

KEEPING A FOOD DIARY

This is a useful exercise, both as an initial reminder of which foods you eat and when you eat them, and in order to find out whether you are achieving a healthy, balanced diet. It is also advisable when you are following an exclusion or elimination diet.

The food diary can help you discover if you really do have a true food intolerance or sensitivity, or whether your symptoms may have other, non food-related causes. Stress, tiredness and even the menstrual cycle

can all aggravate a condition. Write down everything that you eat and drink, any symptoms that appear, and when or if they worsen.

A detailed food diary will also be a helpful aid for your doctor or dietician when they are trying to reach a diagnosis and may help them see where to make any dietary adjustments. Remember that symptoms may not appear immediately after eating an offending food. Any reaction may happen hours – or even days – later. You can't presume that the culprit is something you ate at your last meal. In addition, a sensitivity reaction to food may be worse one day than another. All this makes the detection process quite difficult so you will need to be both vigilant and patient.

THE HEALTHY DIET

Eating a healthy, well-balanced diet can help us to feel more energetic and improve both our short-term and long-term health. Before deciding to cut out foods from your diet because of a food allergy or intolerance, it is important to check that you have been eating a healthy diet. Sometimes, symptoms that are thought to be due to allergies clear up when the overall diet is improved.

Healthy eating doesn't just mean cutting down on foods that are high in fat, sugar or salt. A healthy diet is all about balance and variety. Foods can be grouped according to the essential nutrients they contain. To provide the body with the essential nutrients it needs, eat a variety of foods from each of these food groups, in appropriate amounts, every day. This is an easy way of making sure you are eating a healthy, well-balanced diet. For most people, this means eating more fruit and vegetables and cutting down on foods containing fat and foods containing sugar.

FRUIT AND VEGETABLES
Foods in this group include fresh, frozen and canned fruit and vegetables, dried fruits and fruit and vegetable juices. These foods provide a rich supply of nutrients, such as vitamins, betacarotene, folate and fibre.

Try to eat five or more portions of fruit and vegetables a day. In places where large amounts of fruit and vegetables are eaten every day, such as Mediterranean countries, the incidence of heart disease, cancer and other degenerative diseases is relatively low. Fruit and vegetables are believed to help protect against these diseases.

Above: Starchy foods, such as plantain, yam, sweet potatoes and potatoes, should be included in every meal.

STARCHY FOODS
Foods in this group include bread, potatoes, pasta, rice, noodles, couscous, oats, polenta and breakfast cereals (especially wholegrain varieties). These foods provide vitamins, especially B vitamins; nutrients and minerals, such as calcium and iron; fibre, particularly from wholegrain foods; and energy. Try to include a food from this group at every meal, choosing wholegrain varieties whenever possible.

MILK AND DAIRY FOODS
Foods in this group include milk, cheese, yogurt and fromage frais. They are rich in vitamins B_{12}, A and D; calcium; and protein. Try to include two to three portions of dairy products every day, choosing lower-fat varieties whenever possible. Low-fat varieties contain just as much calcium.

Left: Fruit and vegetables are a valuable source of vitamins and essential nutrients.

How to Boost your Daily Intake of Fruit and Vegetables

Try adding an extra portion to your daily diet and gradually build up to a target of five or more portions a day.

BREAKFAST
• Add fresh or dried fruit to breakfast cereal, e.g. sliced banana, raisins or apricots.
• Have half a grapefruit or canned grapefruit segments in fruit juice.
• Include a glass of fruit juice with your breakfast.
• For a cooked breakfast, try grilled mushrooms on toast.

MAIN MEALS
• Try to include at least two different lightly cooked vegetables with main meals.
• Add frozen vegetables, such as peas, sweetcorn or mixed vegetables to rice or pasta, while it is cooking.
• Add vegetables or fruit (such as dried apricots or apple) to stews or casseroles.

SNACK MEALS
• Always add salad or other vegetables to sandwiches.
• Fresh fruit is the perfect convenient snack – enjoy it on its own or add to other foods, such as plain or fruit yogurt.
• Fingers of raw vegetables, such as peppers, celery and carrots, make a tasty snack when served with a salsa, yogurt or cheese dip.

MEAT, FISH AND ALTERNATIVES
Foods in this group include meat, fish, poultry, eggs, nuts, beans and pulses. These foods provide a good supply of B vitamins, especially B_{12}, iron, magnesium, zinc, and protein. Try to eat two to three portions of foods from this group every day. Choose lean meat, poultry and game and opt for healthy, low-fat cooking methods, such as grilling, steaming and stir-frying. Try to eat oily fish at least twice a week. Beans, such as canned baked beans and peas and lentils, are all low in fat, and have the added advantage of being high in fibre, so try to include some of these foods as often as you can.

FATS AND OILS
This group includes foods such as vegetable oils and fat spreads. These can be included in small amounts every day to provide fat-soluble vitamins and some essential fats which your body cannot make. However, these foods are high in calories, so limit your intake.

FATTY AND SUGARY FOODS
Foods in this group include cakes, biscuits, commercial savoury snacks, sweets, salad dressings and soft drinks. Your consumption of these foods should be limited, as they are usually high in fat, sugar and calories and tend to be less nourishing than other foods. Consider these as "occasional" foods that should be eaten in moderation.

Above: Milk and dairy foods are rich in certain vitamins and minerals but can also have very high levels of saturated fat.

Above: Meat and fish provide a good supply of B vitamins, iron, magnesium and protein.

THE BENEFITS OF EATING FIVE OR MORE PORTIONS OF FRUIT AND VEGETABLES A DAY

• Eating a variety of different fruits and vegetables every day will help you get maximum nutritional benefit.
• They are low in fat and calories so you needn't worry about your weight.
• These foods are packed full of essential vitamins and minerals.
• Brightly coloured vegetables and fruits, and dark green vegetables, are our main source of antioxidants: compounds which help protect us from heart disease and some cancers.
• They are an excellent source of dietary fibre – essential for a healthy digestive system.
• Fruits and vegetables of all varieties add flavour, texture, colour and taste to almost any meal or snack.

TIPS TO STOP VITAMINS BEING LOST FROM FRUIT AND VEGETABLES

• Prepare fruit and vegetables as near to the time for cooking and serving as possible.
• Avoid preparing vegetables in advance and leaving them to soak in water.
• Steam, microwave or lightly boil vegetables in just enough water to cover them, and then serve immediately.
• Keep vegetables in the fridge when possible.
• Try to serve raw fruit and vegetables on a regular basis.
• Where possible, eat fruit and vegetables with the skins on.

THE BENEFITS OF EATING A HEALTHY, WHOLEFOOD DIET

• Eating well will help you to get the most out of life.
• You will gain better control of your weight, without having to diet or count calories.
• There is a lower risk of developing degenerative diseases, such as heart disease and some types of cancer.
• The risk of developing various bowel disorders and osteoporosis is also reduced.
• Tooth decay and gum disease should be less of a problem.
• You will feel more energetic and feel and look more vibrant.

ORGANIC FOODS

These are foods that have been produced without the use of chemicals or artificial fertilizers. There are strict rules governing the production of organic foods, and these are monitored by certification bodies to ensure that manufacturers and farmers comply.

Organic foods are more costly to produce, so are more expensive to buy. However, in recent years there has been a rapid growth in this sector of the market as consumer interest and demand have increased. This has meant greater availability and choice in some supermarkets, which should result in more competitive prices. The range of organic produce has expanded from fruit and vegetables to include meat, dairy products (especially milk), cereal products, wines and beers.

The trend for organic products appears to be continuing to grow, as people become more aware of the health implications surrounding the way in which foods are produced.

Left: With an increased demand for organic produce, supermarkets are now offering a wider range of organic foods.

MAINTAINING A
HEALTHY BALANCE

If you are embarking on a diet which potentially cuts out some of the major food groups, and therefore the nutrients they provide, it is important that you include alternative dietary sources, so that the nutritional quality of your diet is maintained.

For example, if milk and dairy foods – the major source of calcium in the diet – are to be avoided, suitable alternatives must be included to ensure the body receives enough calcium for good health. Thankfully, there are alternatives, particularly in the form of calcium-fortified soya milks and foods made from these, which are becoming increasingly popular and are found in major supermarkets. People with coeliac disease sometimes worry that, because they are unable to eat wheat and wheat bran, they may not be getting enough fibre in their diet. Once again, alternatives need to be included, for example wholegrain rice, beans and pulses, and plenty of fresh fruit and vegetables, with the skins on. Commercially produced high-fibre, gluten-free foods are also available.

Cutting out eggs or fish from the diet is less of a problem nutritionally, because these foods can easily be replaced. However, it can be quite difficult to establish which processed foods contain egg.

It is usually possible, therefore, to maintain a healthy, well-balanced diet, even when some staple foods are excluded. Clearly, the more restricted you are in terms of which foods you can eat, the harder it is to ensure a proper nutritional balance, and the more planning and effort it will take to ensure a healthy diet. This book will provide all the advice and information you may need about various special diets, along with a huge choice of delicious recipes to suit your needs.

Below: If you have to cut out certain foods from your diet, it is important to include a wide range of foods to maintain a healthy balance of nutrients.

GLUTEN AND COELIAC DISEASE

If you are reading this chapter, the chances are that you, or someone close to you, has been advised to follow a gluten-free diet. The most likely reason for this is a diagnosis of coeliac disease, but you may have a wheat allergy or a relatively rare skin condition. Whatever the reason, being faced with following a diet for life may seem rather daunting. The good news is that gluten is not particularly difficult to avoid: a huge range of delicious foods remains open to you and you won't need to be singled out from family or friends as everything you eat can be enjoyed by them, too.

WHAT IS GLUTEN?

Gluten is a protein that occurs naturally in wheat and rye and is closely related to similar proteins in oats and barley. When the grain is milled, it is the gluten that gives the flour its strength and elasticity. Most people ingest gluten without any difficulty, but in some individuals, it can cause problems.

COELIAC DISEASE

This lifelong condition, caused by a sensitivity to gluten, affects about one in 1,000 to one in 1,500 people world-wide. Coeliac disease was once thought of as a disease exclusive to childhood, but while the condition is present from birth, the symptoms may not appear until much later in life. Nowadays, far more adults than children have the condition; the majority of newly diagnosed coeliacs are aged between 30 and 45, with a significant number falling in the over-60s category.

The condition is known to run in families, and some coeliacs without obvious symptoms are detected when their relatives are being studied. It is suspected that many cases of coeliac disease remain undiagnosed, so the number of cases may in fact be higher.

Coeliac disease was first recognized by the Greeks in the 2nd century AD; the word "coeliac" is derived from the Greek word "koiliakos", meaning "suffering in the bowels", an apt description of a condition that affects the gastrointestinal tract.

In a person with a healthy digestive system, food that has been broken down in the stomach and duodenum passes through the small intestine, where thread-like projections called villi absorb essential nutrients.

SYMPTOMS

The symptoms of coeliac disease vary widely, and can be attributable to other medical conditions, so it is vital to seek a proper diagnosis before starting a gluten-free diet.

An adult with coeliac disease may be chronically tired (often due to anaemia resulting from poor iron and folic acid absorption). Mouth ulcers are common, as is abdominal discomfort, often with a feeling of fullness or bloating. Sufferers can be very ill indeed, with vomiting, diarrhoea and severe weight loss. There may be a long history of stomach upsets, or the onset may have been sudden.

The symptoms of coeliac disease may become apparent at any age. In a baby, for instance, the first sign of a problem is usually about three months, when the child is being weaned. If a child who previously enjoyed his or her feeds becomes miserable at mealtimes, refuses foods and stops gaining weight, medical advice should be sought.

If undiagnosed and untreated, a baby with the coeliac condition will lose weight, become listless and irritable and develop a swollen pot-belly. The stools will be unusually pale, with an offensive odour, and there may be diarrhoea and vomiting. If the condition persists, the child will eventually become seriously ill.

Left: Seek medical advice before you or one of your family starts a gluten-free diet.

When someone who suffers from coeliac disease eats food containing gluten, the intestine responds to the food as if it were a foreign body. There is an immune response: the lining of the intestine becomes inflamed and this causes the villi to become flattened. As a result, the surface area is reduced and the gut is no longer able to absorb nutrients efficiently. Over time, weight loss and wasting can occur, leading to malnutrition.

Precisely how or why gluten is harmful to the small intestine is not known, but the only cure for the diagnosed coeliac is to follow a strict gluten-free diet for life. Once gluten is withdrawn from the diet, the flattened villi in the lining of the small intestine will gradually return to normal. Gluten can never be reintroduced, however; once the body has become sensitized to gluten, it will always be affected by it. The occasional minor slip-up may only have a minimal effect, but if the diet is not followed strictly and even small quantities of foods containing gluten are eaten regularly, the unpleasant symptoms will return, causing severe discomfort as well as further damage to the delicate intestine.

If you are uncertain as to whether a given food contains gluten, avoid it. It is simply not worth taking the risk.

When an individual embarks upon a gluten-free diet, the results are sometimes dramatic, but more often he or she will see a gradual but continuing improvement. It takes time for the lining of the small intestine to grow again.

Some coeliacs find that very fatty foods irritate their stomachs; these are often best avoided, particularly in the early stages of the diet. However, it is important not to lose sight of the fact that everyone suffers from illness at some time and a coeliac who feels under the weather may simply have succumbed to a bug that is doing the rounds; before jumping to conclusions, consult a doctor.

WHEAT ALLERGY OR WHEAT INTOLERANCE AND DERMATITIS HERPETIFORMIS

A strict gluten-free diet may also prove beneficial to people who suffer from an allergy or intolerance to wheat, as well as anyone suffering from the rare and irritating skin complaint known as dermatitis herpetiformis.

Wheat allergy or intolerance can cause a wide range of symptoms including aches and pains in the joints and muscles, coughing, sneezing, runny nose, watery and itchy eyes, skin rashes, eczema, faintness and dizziness. The sufferer may have a swollen throat or tongue and find it difficult to swallow. Chest pains, palpitations, nausea, vomiting, diarrhoea, tiredness, lethargy, depression and mood swings have also been reported. Of course, all of these symptoms can be indicative of a range of conditions, and sufferers should always seek sound medical advice before assuming that wheat is the culprit.

If the sufferer's suspicions are confirmed, however, he or she should exclude all sources of wheat, including wheat protein and wheat starch. Some sufferers may also have an allergic reaction to other grains, such as rye, corn and barley, but unlike coeliacs, many people who are allergic to wheat can still tolerate oats.

A product labelled as being gluten-free may also be wheat-free, but this is not inevitable; there may certainly be no gluten present, but the product may contain wheat starch. Always check the packaging or seek more information.

Dermatitis herpetiformis – also caused by a sensitivity to gluten – is a rare skin condition that causes an extremely itchy skin rash that consists of red raised patches and small blisters, appearing most often on the elbows, buttocks and knees. The first appearance of the skin rash most often occurs in people who are aged between 15 and 40. The condition is rare in children, although the symptoms can appear at any age.

Dermatitis herpetiformis affects about 1 in 20,000 people (slightly more males than females) and must be diagnosed by a specialist in skin diseases.

Because gluten is implicated, people who suffer from dermatitis herpetiformis may also have coeliac disease, although in these people the symptoms will usually be quite mild. A permanent gluten-free diet will alleviate both the skin condition and the mild version of coeliac disease, although it may take some time for the skin rash to disappear entirely.

DIAGNOSIS

Whether the sufferer is an adult or a child, it is vital that the coeliac condition is properly diagnosed by a doctor before a gluten-free diet is embarked upon.

Diagnosis is by a standard test – a jejunal biopsy – performed under light sedation in the outpatient department of a hospital. A gastroenterologist will remove a small piece of the villi from the lining of the small intestine. Microscopic examination will reveal whether or not the coeliac condition is present.

If the diagnosis is positive, all the patient needs to do to restore the intestine to health is to adhere strictly to a full and varied gluten-free diet. In the short term, the doctor may decide to prescribe a course of vitamins or mineral supplements.

WHICH FOODS CONTAIN GLUTEN?

A gluten-free diet excludes all foods containing any form of wheat, barley, rye and oats. (Some coeliacs can tolerate oats with no adverse effects, but many cannot, so it is a wise precaution to exclude it.) Items such as bread, cakes, biscuits, pasta and pastries made from wheat flour are obvious sources of gluten, but it is also essential to be aware of less obvious sources, as when wheat flour has been used to coat or dust foods or thicken soups, stews, gravies and puddings. Breadcrumbs, for instance, are used in stuffings and coatings or as a filler in foods such as sausages and hamburgers.

FOODS THAT ARE NATURALLY GLUTEN-FREE

• Fresh or frozen plain meat, fish or poultry, without stuffing or a crumb coating; canned or pre-packed plain cooked meats, such as corned beef or ham (without any coating); smoked and cured pure meats; fresh, frozen or cured plain fish or shellfish; fish canned in oil, brine or water.

Above: Anchovies canned in oil, smoked mackerel and cooked prawns, are all naturally gluten-free.

• Fresh or frozen plain vegetables or fruit, dried fruit and vegetables (including pulses), plain canned fruit in syrup or juice, vegetables canned in brine, water or juice, plain vegetables pickled in vinegar, potato crisps.
• Eggs (but not Scotch eggs).
• Nuts and seeds of all types, provided they are plain; also peanut butter.
• Gelatine and agar agar.
• Dairy produce including all plain cheeses (but not spreads or processed cheese), milk, dairy cream, natural yogurt, fromage frais; also plain dried milk, evaporated and condensed milk.
• Fats and oils, including pure vegetable oils, such as olive, sunflower and rapeseed; butter, margarine (as long as it does not contain wheatgerm oil), reduced-fat and low-fat spreads.
• Sugar in all its forms, including pure honey, syrup, molasses and treacle.
• Fruit conserves, jam and marmalade.
• Flavourings, seasonings, herbs and spices, including salt, freshly ground black pepper, black peppercorns, cider vinegar and wine vinegar, pure whole or ground spices, tomato purée and garlic purée, pure food flavourings, such as vanilla and almond essences, pure food colourings.
• Breakfast cereals, such as rice crispies, puffed rice, some cornflakes.

Above: Breakfast need not be a problem for coeliacs. Eggs, jam or marmalade, milk and rice- and corn-based cereals, such as rice crispies and some cornflakes, are all gluten-free. Serve them with gluten-free toast.

Above: Add flavour and colour to your meals using black peppercorns, tomato purée, red wine vinegar, pure ground cinnamon, pure food flavourings and colourings.

• Grains, whether whole or ground, including buckwheat flakes and flour, carob flour, cornflour, gram flour (from ground chick-peas), maize flour, millet flour, potato flour, sorghum flour, soya flour, sweet chestnut flour, teff flour, yam flour, yellow split pea flour, arrowroot, rice (all types including wild rice; also ground rice and rice flour), hominy grits, millet (also millet flakes and millet seeds), polenta, quinoa grains, sago and tapioca.
• Good quality plain chocolate.
• Yeast (and yeast extract).
• Pure rice noodles, pure corn, rice and millet pasta, pure buckwheat pasta – check that pastas do not contain added wheat flour, starch or binders.
• Drinks, such as tea, coffee, fruit squashes (except barley water), pure fruit juices (preferably unsweetened); also cider, wine, sherry, brandy, port.

MANUFACTURED FOODS THAT ARE GLUTEN-FREE

A wide range of specially manufactured gluten-free foods is also available. The list includes breads, cakes, biscuits, crackers and crispbreads, plus flours, flour mixes, bread and cake mixes, muesli, pastas and rusks. Talk to your doctor, as in certain countries, such as the UK, you may be able to obtain some of these products on prescription. Others can be purchased from chemists or health food shops, or by mail order, although they can be costly.

Manufactured foods that have been specifically made for the market by reputable companies are very useful. They look like the wheat-flour products they are intended to replace, so will go unremarked at occasions such as children's parties.

Many everyday canned and packaged foods are also gluten-free.

When using products, such as gluten-free flours or bread or cake mixes for the first time, always follow the manufacturer's guidance and instructions on usage.

FOODS TO AVOID

The following foods always contain flour made from wheat, barley, rye or oats, so must be avoided:
• Wheat berries or grains; wheat bran; wheat flakes; wheat flour, such as plain or strong white flour, brown, granary and wholemeal flours; wheat-meal; wheat protein; wheat starch; bulgur wheat; couscous; cracked wheat, durum wheat (used in pasta); kibbled wheat; pourgouri; rusk; semolina; wheatgerm.
• Pearl barley, pot barley, barley flakes, barley flour, barley meal.
• Rye flakes, rye flour, rye meal.
• Oats, oat flakes, jumbo oats, porridge oats, rolled oats, oatmeal, pinhead oatmeal, oatbran, oatgerm.
• Spelt (flour and American pasta made from a grain related to wheat), kamut (Italian wholegrain pasta).
• Triticale (wheat/rye hybrid grain).

COMMON FOODS THAT MAY CONTAIN GLUTEN

• Dry goods like baking powder, malt, curry powder, mustard powder, MSG (monosodium glutamate flavour enhancer), gravy mixes, spices and spice mixes, pepper compounds and ready-ground white pepper, shredded suet (in packets), stock cubes.
• Pasta (durum wheat pastas are out and some Oriental pastas, though made from other grains, contain wheat).
• Some cornflakes.
• Salad dressings, soy sauce, malt vinegar.
• Some processed cheese spreads, some flavoured yogurts.
• Sausages (and sausage rolls), meat pies, beefburgers, pâtés, foods coated in batter or breadcrumbs.
• Dry roasted nuts.
• Communion wafers (gluten-free wafers are available on mail-order).
• Beers, malted milk drinks.

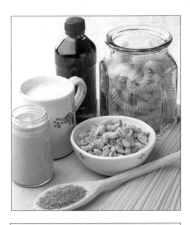

Above right: Some common foods, such as malt vinegar, pasta made with wheat, dry roasted nuts, mustards and malted milk drinks, contain gluten and must be avoided.

Below: The range of specially manufactured gluten-free foods includes biscuits, cereal, corn pasta and gluten-free flours.

FOOD LABELLING

By law, all manufacturers have to mark or label food with a list of ingredients. Sources of gluten are not always obvious, however. If you read any of the following words on a food label, alarm bells should start to ring and you should ask for more information: binder, binding, cereal, cereal protein, corn, cornstarch, edible starch, flour, food starch, modified starch, rusk, special edible starch, starch, thickener, thickening or vegetable protein.

GLUTEN-FREE COOKING

There is nothing special about gluten-free cooking other than the fact that some ingredients are replaced with alternatives that are equally varied and interesting. Once you familiarize yourself with the list of foods that can safely be served (and note the no-no's), it is simply a matter of making delicious dishes that everyone can enjoy. You will rapidly get into the habit of using a variety of alternative starches for baking, cooking, thickening, binding and coating, and in doing so will discover just how delicious many of the less familiar grains can be.

If you are new to gluten-free cooking, you will probably prefer to start with simple no-risk dishes like grills with fresh vegetables. This will have obvious health advantages, but don't turf out the treats. If you continue to serve pies and puddings, cakes and bakes, but make them gluten-free, everyone in the family will be able to enjoy their favourite foods – and the coeliac won't feel isolated.

USING GLUTEN-FREE FLOURS

Because gluten is the protein that strengthens and binds dough in baking, you may need to find alternative binding agents when using gluten-free flours. Follow recipes for baked goods closely, as they will have been specially formulated to allow for this potential problem. A combination of starches often works better than a single type, and adding egg, pectin powder, grated apple or mashed banana may help to bind gluten-free dough.

BINDING BURGERS AND SAUSAGES

Although burgers and sausages are usually bound with breadcrumbs or rusk, they work equally well without. The best hamburgers are made purely from minced steak, and fresh sausage meat will hold together without additional ingredients. If you must use a binder, add rice flour and egg.

AVOIDING WHEAT CONTAMINATION

If you are baking a batch of breads, cakes and pastries (only some of which are gluten-free), be careful to keep ingredients separate so that there is no risk of wheat flour contaminating the gluten-free foods. Wash all utensils thoroughly after each use. For a highly allergic person, it may be sensible to use separate baking tins and cooking utensils. Alternatively – and this is simpler and safer – use gluten-free ingredients for all your cooking.

QUICK TIPS ON GLUTEN-FREE COOKING

• Do not use breadcrumbs (unless they are gluten-free) for coating foods. Crushed gluten-free cornflakes make a good alternative for coating foods and for gratins.

• Roll gluten-free pastry out on greaseproof paper as this makes it easier to lift and to line the tin.

• If gluten-free pastry is very crumbly, press it over the base and up the sides of the tin (as when making shortbread) rather than trying to roll it out.

• Do not dust or coat foods with wheat flour prior to cooking – either avoid dusting food altogether or use naturally gluten-free flours such as maize meal or rice flour.

• Grease baking tins before use, even if they are non-stick, or line the tins with non-stick baking parchment to prevent sticking.

• It is a good idea to bake a batch of gluten-free breads, cakes and biscuits and pop some into the freezer. Gluten-free baked goods freeze well and will keep fresh for many weeks. Freeze in portions, so that you can thaw exactly what you need for a packed lunch or tea-time treat.

• Potato flour is a useful thickening agent for gravies, stews, casseroles, sauces and soups.

STORE-CUPBOARD ESSENTIALS

Pack your pantry with these items and you'll always have the makings of a gluten-free meal:

- Gluten-free cornflakes, rice crispies, puffed rice cereal.
- Fish, such as anchovies, sardines or tuna, canned in oil, brine or water.
- Canned cooked meat, such as ham or gluten-free corned beef.
- Vegetables canned in water, brine or juice, pickled vegetables.
- Dried vegetables and pulses, plain potato crisps.
- Canned fruit in syrup or juice.
- Plain dried fruit, glacé cherries.
- Fruit juices and squashes (except barley water).
- Rice; also rice noodles and other gluten-free pastas.
- Plain nuts (not dry roasted) and seeds, pure peanut butter.
- Sugars, pure syrups, pure honey, jam, marmalade.
- Dried plain milk, evaporated and condensed milk, tea, pure coffee, good quality plain chocolate.

- Naturally gluten-free flours, which include rice flour, maize flour or maize meal, gluten-free cornflour, potato flour and soya flour; also yeast.
- Ground rice, tapioca, buckwheat flakes, millet flakes, rice flakes.
- Gelatine or agar agar.
- Pure vegetable oils, wine vinegar or cider vinegar.
- Salt, black peppercorns, dried herbs, pure spices.
- Pure food flavourings and colourings.
- Tomato purée, garlic purée, gluten-free soy sauce.

Above: Essential store-cupboard items should include: rice cakes, polenta, pure spices, dried herbs, gluten-free cornflour, rice noodles, rice and gluten-free flour.

Left: Stock up on naturally gluten-free foods, such as jams and marmalades, canned fruits and vegetables, pickled onions, crisps, dried fruit and gluten-free breakfast cereals.

GLUTEN-FREE ACCOMPANIMENTS

Potatoes and rice are particularly good sources of natural, gluten-free carbohydrate. They make ideal accompaniments to many dishes and can be served in a wide variety of ways. Explore the potential of gluten-free pastas, too. Rice noodles and corn pasta are delicious, and polenta is very good with sauced dishes; try it freshly cooked or cooled, cut into wedges and shallow fried.

POTATOES

There are few vegetables as versatile as potatoes. Tiny new potatoes are very good boiled or steamed, baked potatoes make a meal in themselves with a tasty topping, and home-made chips are one treat a gluten-free diet doesn't deny you. Patties, cakes or croquettes, rolled in crushed gluten-free cornflakes or breadcrumbs, make an excellent accompaniment, and mashed potatoes can be served in numerous ways. Always use the right variety of potato for the job. Scrub potatoes and leave the skins on when roasting or making chips for extra texture, flavour and fibre. For a tasty change, try either sweet potatoes or yams.

RICE

There are many different varieties of rice including brown and white, long grain, short grain, pudding rice, basmati and risotto rice (arborio), all of which are gluten-free, as is wild rice. Boiled rice can be served as it is, stir-fried or used as the basis for a salad.

Above: Potatoes, sweet potatoes and yams are all naturally gluten-free.

Below: Don't just opt for plain boiled long grain rice, try cooking wild rice, wholegrain rice or risotto rice, for a change.

RICE NOODLES

These are made from ground rice and water and range in thickness from very thin to wide ribbons and sheets. They are available fresh or dried and are often soaked in warm water before being briefly cooked.

CORN PASTA

Pure corn pasta – made from maize without added binders or starch – is ideal for a gluten-free diet. It comes in a variety of flavours (including parsley, spinach and chilli) and in shapes that range from spaghetti to twists and shells. All versions look pretty on the plate and have a good flavour. Corn pasta makes an excellent alternative to durum wheat pasta.

Above: Corn pasta, rice noodles and polenta make marvellous accompaniments.

POLENTA

Coarsely ground maize, this is a staple food in Italy, where it is often served as an accompaniment instead of rice or pasta. The partly cooked ground grain is whisked into boiling water or stock.

HOW TO COOK POLENTA

Bring 1.2 litres/2 pints/5 cups salted water or stock to the boil in a large saucepan, then sprinkle 175g/6oz/generous 1 cup polenta into the water, stirring continuously. Cook, uncovered, over a very low heat for about 40 minutes, stirring frequently, until cooked and thick. Season and add flavourings, such as cheese, butter, garlic and herbs. Serve hot.

HOW TO COOK BROWN RICE

Bring 1.4 litres/2¼ pints/5⅔ cups lightly salted water to the boil in a large saucepan. Add 250g/9oz/1¼ cups brown rice. Bring back to the boil, then lower the heat and allow to simmer, uncovered, for 25–35 minutes until the rice is tender but retains a bit of bite. Drain in a sieve, rinse with boiling water, then drain thoroughly again.

HOW TO COOK RICE NOODLES

Bring 2 litres/4½ pints/8 cups lightly salted water to the boil in a large saucepan. Turn off the heat and add 250g/9oz/2¼ cups rice noodles. Stir the noodles with a fork to separate them, cover and set aside for 4 minutes. Drain and serve. If serving the noodles cold, rinse in cold water and drain again.

GLUTEN-FREE SNACKS AND FINGER FOODS

We all enjoy snacks at some time, particularly when the munchies strike. When baking, make extra gluten-free cakes and biscuits and freeze the surplus in slices. That way, you can thaw individual portions as needed. Occasional treats, such as a bar of gluten-free chocolate or a packet of plain crisps, won't do any harm, but it is useful to have a good selection of healthy and delicious gluten-free snacks and treats available, ready to keep hunger pangs at bay.
• Fresh fruit, such as apples, pears, mangoes, kiwi fruit, pineapple wedges, peaches, apricots and oranges.
• Ready-to-eat dried fruit, such as apricots, peaches, pears, apples, prunes or dried fruit salad.
• Gluten-free crackers, crispbreads and rice cakes. Serve them with plain cheese, such as Cheddar, Red Leicester, Stilton or Emmental.
• Wedges of gluten-free fruit cake.

• Plain nuts, such as walnuts, almonds or hazelnuts or a mixture of nuts and dried fruit, mixed seeds or a mixture of mixed seeds and plain nuts.
• Plain yogurt to which you can add chopped fresh fruit for a sweet treat, or finely diced cucumber and a trace of

Above: Healthy gluten-free snacks include nuts, mixed nuts and raisins, cheese and rice crackers, and raw vegetable crudités.

crushed garlic for a savoury surprise; also plain or flavoured fromage frais and gluten-free fruit yogurts.

Basic Gluten-free Recipes

There is a wide range of stock products on the market including cubes of various flavours, stock powders or granules and fresh chilled stock, but some of these contain gluten, so it is worthwhile making your own gluten-free stocks at home. Home-made stocks add delicious flavour to many different dishes, and they really are simple to make. It is a good idea to prepare one or two batches and freeze them in useful quantities for future use. Cool home-made stocks quickly, pour them into suitable containers (leaving space for expansion) and freeze them for up to 3 months.

CHICKEN STOCK
Makes about 750ml/1¼ pints/3 cups
1 meaty chicken carcass
6 shallots or 1 onion
1 carrot
2 celery sticks
1 bay leaf
salt and ground black pepper

1 Break or chop the chicken carcass into pieces and place in a large saucepan with 1.75 litres/3 pints/7½ cups cold water.

2 Peel and slice the shallots or onion and carrot, then chop the celery. Add the vegetables to the saucepan with the bayleaf. Stir to mix.

3 Bring to the boil, then partially cover and simmer for 2 hours, skimming off any scum and fat that rises to the surface during cooking.

4 Strain the stock through a sieve, then set aside to cool.

5 When cold, remove and discard all the fat and use the stock or freeze. Once cool, cover and store in the fridge for up to 3 days. Season with salt and pepper, as required.

BEEF STOCK
Makes about 750ml/1¼ pints/3 cups
450g/1lb shin of beef on the bone
450g/1lb beef or veal bones
1 onion
1 carrot
1 turnip
2 celery sticks
1 leek
1 bouquet garni
salt and ground black pepper

1 Preheat the oven to 220°C/425°F/Gas 7. Place the meat and bones in a roasting tin and brown in the oven for about 30 minutes, then place in a large pan with 1.75 litres/3 pints/7½ cups cold water.

2 Peel and slice the onion and carrot, then peel and dice the turnip and chop the celery and leek. Add the vegetables to the saucepan with the bouquet garni. Stir to mix.

3 Bring to the boil, then partially cover and simmer for 2 hours, skimming off any scum and fat that rises to the surface during cooking. Strain the stock through a fine sieve, then set aside to cool. Store as for chicken stock.

VEGETABLE STOCK
Makes about 1.5 litres/2½ pints/6¼ cups
1 large onion, sliced
2 carrots, sliced
1 leek, sliced
3 celery sticks, chopped
1 small turnip, diced
1 small parsnip, sliced
1 bouquet garni
salt and ground black pepper

1 Place all the prepared vegetables in a large saucepan with the bouquet garni. Add 1.75 litres/3 pints/7½ cups cold water and stir to mix.

2 Bring to the boil, then partially cover and simmer for about 1 hour, skimming off any scum.

3 Strain the stock through a sieve, use immediately or set aside to cool. Store in the fridge for up to 3 days. Alternatively, freeze the stock. Season with salt and pepper, as required.

COOK'S TIP
If you have any vegetable trimmings, such as tomato or onion skins, celery tops or cabbage leaves, then add these to the water with the vegetables when making the stock.

GLUTEN-FREE WHITE SAUCE
Makes about 300ml/¹/₂ pint/1¹/₄ cups
30ml/2 tbsp gluten-free cornflour
300ml/½ pint/1¼ cups semi-
　skimmed milk
15g/½oz/1 tbsp sunflower
　margarine
salt and ground black pepper

1 Place the cornflour in a bowl and
　blend with 60ml/4 tbsp of the milk
to make a smooth paste.

2 Heat the remaining milk in a
　saucepan over a medium heat until
boiling, then pour on to the blended
mixture, whisking continuously to
prevent lumps forming.

3 Return the mixture to the
　saucepan and bring slowly to the
boil, stirring continuously, until the
sauce thickens. Lower the heat and
simmer gently for 2–3 minutes, then
stir in the margarine, until melted.
Season to taste and serve.

VARIATIONS
● To make a thinner pouring sauce,
reduce the quantity of cornflour to
20–25ml/4–5 tsp.
● Replace half the milk with well-
flavoured vegetable or chicken stock or
use a half-and-half mixture of stock
and white wine in place of the milk.
● Add gluten-free flavourings, such as
grated cheese, chopped mixed fresh
herbs, lightly sautéed onions, tomato
purée, or chopped or sliced, cooked
wild or button mushrooms, to the
sauce for extra flavour.

FRENCH DRESSING
Makes about 150ml/¹/₄ pint/²/₃ cup
90ml/6 tbsp sunflower oil
30ml/2 tbsp white wine vinegar or
　lemon juice
5ml/1 tsp Dijon mustard
1.5ml/¼ tsp caster sugar
15ml/1 tbsp chopped fresh
　mixed herbs
salt and ground black pepper

1 Place all the ingredients in a small
　bowl and whisk together until
thoroughly mixed. Alternatively, place
all the ingredients in a clean, screw-
top jar, seal and shake well until
thoroughly mixed.

2 Adjust the seasoning and serve
　immediately or keep in a screw-top
jar in the fridge for up to 1 week.
Shake thoroughly before serving.

VARIATIONS
● Crush a small garlic clove and add to
the dressing, if you like.
● Use light olive oil in place of some
or all of the sunflower oil.
● Try balsamic vinegar in place of the
white wine vinegar.

MAYONNAISE
Makes about 200ml/7fl oz/scant 1 cup
2 egg yolks
5ml/1 tsp Dijon mustard
15ml/1 tbsp lemon juice
2.5ml/½ tsp salt
ground black pepper
about 150ml/¼ pint/²/₃ cup olive or
　sunflower oil

1 Place the egg yolks, mustard, lemon
　juice, salt, pepper and 15ml/1 tbsp
oil in a food processor or small blender.
Blend for 30 seconds.

2 With the motor running, gradually
　add the remaining oil, pouring it
through the funnel in a slow, steady
stream, until the mayonnaise is thick,
creamy and smooth.

3 Adjust the seasoning, then use
　immediately or cover and chill
until required. Store for up to 3 days
in a covered container in the fridge.

VARIATIONS
Add finely chopped garlic, capers,
gherkins or cucumber, crumbled blue
cheese or chopped fresh mixed herbs.

MILK AND DAIRY PRODUCTS

Some people choose a dairy-free diet for either moral or religious reasons, but others have the decision made for them when they develop an intolerance or an allergy to cow's milk. Whatever your reason for omitting cow's milk and its products from your diet, you can still enjoy a wide range of varied and delicious meals. All it takes is a little planning. This book includes plenty of help, advice and information, plus lots of tasty dairy-free recipes for you, your friends and family to enjoy, from soups and starters to main courses, desserts, cakes and bakes.

WHAT EXACTLY ARE DAIRY FOODS?

We all know what dairy foods are, don't we? Maybe not. There is actually quite a lot of confusion about this term. Essentially, it applies to cow's milk, cream, butter, cheese and related items like buttermilk, yogurt, fromage frais and dairy ice cream. Many processed foods contain milk and dairy products. Obvious candidates are milk chocolate and dairy spreads, but there are many other items, too, such as biscuits, cakes, breads, breakfast cereals, pancake and batter mixes, pudding mixes, instant hot chocolate drinks and coffee whiteners.

ARE WE ONLY SPEAKING ABOUT COW'S MILK?

Technically, when we refer to dairy foods, this really only means cow's milk and products derived from cow's milk. Goat's milk and ewe's milk – and foods derived from them, such as cheese and yogurt – are not thought of as dairy foods even though they have a similar composition to cow's milk, and can sometimes cause similar problems for sensitive individuals. Other people who are sensitive to cow's milk, however, are often able to tolerate goat or ewe's milk, and their associated products quite well.

OTHER NAMES FOR MILK AND MILK PRODUCTS

As well as all the foods that we commonly think of as dairy products, such as cheese, yogurt, butter and cream, there are a number of other products that are forms of cow's milk or that have been derived from cow's milk. It is important to look out for these as it is very easy for the uninitiated to miss them and they often crop up in the most unlikely places. It is particularly important to check for them in processed and ready-made foods.

- casein
- caseinates
- ghee
- hydrolyzed casein
- hydrolyzed milk protein
- lactose
- lactalbumin
- milk sugar
- milk solids
- non-fat milk solids
- skimmed milk whey
- skimmed milk powder
- whey
- whey protein
- whey sugar
- whey syrup sweetener

Left: There are a great many cow's milk dairy products, which include (clockwise from top left): milk, evaporated milk, fromage frais, condensed milk, dairy spread, curd cheese, butter, buttermilk and cream, and in the centre, cheese and yogurt.

Left: Regular exercise and a good supply of calcium are needed for strong, healthy bones.

AVERAGE CALCIUM VALUES OF DAIRY AND OTHER MILKS

The daily calcium requirement for the average adult is 700mg. If you are concerned about your calcium intake, use the table below to check that you are getting enough.

Type of milk	Per 100ml
whole cow's milk (including lactose-reduced)	120mg
semi-skimmed and skimmed cow's milk	120–125mg
evaporated milk	290mg
goat's milk	120mg
sheep's milk	170mg
soya milk	13mg
soya milk (with added calcium)	140mg

IS IT OKAY TO GIVE UP MILK?

Before embarking on a dairy-free diet, or even substantially reducing your intake of dairy foods, it is only sensible to seek advice from a doctor or nutritionist. Milk is the most complete food available, providing valuable amounts of protein, fat, carbohydrate (in the form of lactose/milk sugar), vitamin A and – particularly – B_2 (riboflavin). It is rich in readily absorbed calcium and also a good source of phosphorus. In young children, who may be picky about what and how much they eat, milk is often the main source of energy. If you give up milk and other dairy products, whether in the short term or for longer, it is therefore important to look at other ways of providing these nutrients, especially calcium.

THE IMPORTANCE OF CALCIUM IN OUR DIET

Calcium is essential for building strong teeth and bones, normal blood clotting, nerve function and enzyme activity. It is particularly important for young children and teenagers, but even after we stop growing, at around the age of 18 years, the body's need for calcium continues. Requirements for this valuable nutrient are also higher during pregnancy and breastfeeding.

Recent research suggests that having adequate amounts of calcium in early life and building up a strong skeletal structure may help to prevent osteoporosis, or "brittle bone disease" in later life. This condition occurs when calcium is lost faster than it can be replaced, and bones become weak and fragile. Taking regular exercise (especially weight-bearing exercise) also helps to strengthen bones. Vitamin D, which is produced by the action of sunlight on the skin, helps with the absorption of calcium by the body, whereas both smoking and excessive drinking of alcohol deplete calcium reserves.

NON-DAIRY CALCIUM SOURCES

If you are unable to tolerate dairy products, do not despair. Although dairy foods offer a rich and easily absorbable supply of calcium, there are plenty of other foods that can also provide a good supply of the mineral. These include:

• White or brown bread (fortified).
• Leafy dark green vegetables, such as Savoy cabbage, spring greens, curly kale, broccoli and spinach.
• Canned sardines or pilchards in oil or tomato sauce (provided the bones are eaten).
• Canned baked beans in tomato sauce, red kidney beans, chick-peas and lentils.
• Soya beans and tofu (beancurd).
• Nuts, particularly almonds, Brazil nuts and hazelnuts.
• Seeds, such as sesame seeds and sunflower seeds.
• Dried apricots, dried figs and currants.
• muesli

Above: Add extra calcium to your diet by nibbling dried fruit, such as dried figs, or add currants to cakes or dried fruit salads.

Below: Canned sardines are a good source of calcium – as long as you eat the bones.

AVERAGE CALCIUM VALUES OF OTHER FOODS	
Type of food	**Per 100g**
almonds	240mg
apricots, dried	73mg
Brazil nuts	170mg
bread, brown (fortified)	170mg
bread, white (fortified)	110mg
canned baked beans in tomato sauce	48mg
canned sardines (with bones)	500mg
canned pilchards (with bones)	300mg
curly kale, boiled	150mg
figs, dried	230mg
lentils, boiled	22mg
hazelnuts	140mg
muesli, Swiss-style	110mg
red kidney beans, boiled	71mg
Savoy cabbage, boiled	37mg
sesame seeds	670mg
soya beans, boiled	83mg
spinach, boiled	160mg
spring greens, boiled	75mg
sunflower seeds	110mg
tofu (beancurd)	510mg

LACTOSE INTOLERANCE V MILK ALLERGY – WHAT'S THE DIFFERENCE?

LACTOSE INTOLERANCE

This not an allergic reaction but occurs because the body lacks (or does not produce enough of) an enzyme called lactase, which is normally active in the intestinal wall. The function of lactase is to break down lactose (milk sugar) into simpler sugars that can be absorbed by the body. If this doesn't happen, the undigested lactose passes into the large intestine (colon) where it causes irritation and the classic symptoms commonly associated with lactose intolerance. These include bloating, stomach pain, diarrhoea and excessive wind, produced by naturally occurring microflora in the gut, which ferment the undigested lactose and produce gas.

Lactase deficiency is estimated to affect around two-thirds of the world's population. It is more common among non-white/black races, where milk is not a staple food after weaning. However, in Northern Europe, where dairy products are commonly eaten, adults are less likely to have reduced levels of lactase enzyme.

Temporary lactose intolerance can also be triggered by a bout of gastro-enteritis (particularly in young children) or in adults as a consequence of any illness that affects the lining of the small intestine. This sensitivity is generally only short term and usually clears up if the individual avoids cow's milk for a time.

The degree of intolerance varies and may be mild or quite severe. Some people can tolerate small amounts of cow's milk; some find they must avoid drinking milk on its own, but can eat yogurt and some cheeses (which contain little lactose). Some can cope with goat's milk or sheep's milk, although these also contain lactose and can provoke a reaction in susceptible individuals. Other alternative milks, such as soya milk, can also provide suitable substitutes, although for nutritional reasons, establishing an acceptable low level of regular milk is often advised.

MILK ALLERGY

Unlike lactose intolerance, milk allergy is a relatively uncommon condition; and is usually a reaction to the protein (not the lactose) in milk. It is generally restricted to young children, who usually outgrow the problem by the age of two or three. The classic symptoms of an allergy to milk protein are eczema, asthma, allergic rhinitis (a persistent runny nose), vomiting and diarrhoea. In rare instances, the reaction may be severe, and professional

Right: Milk allergy is relatively uncommon and most young children can drink milk.

Below: Although lactase deficiency can affect people from all nationalities, it is more prevalent in black ethnic groups.

guidance should always be sought if an allergy is suspected.

Sometimes, sensitivity to protein and lactose can coexist, particularly after a gastrointestinal upset. The usual treatment is to temporarily exclude milk and dairy products, but again, it is only sensible to seek professional advice from a doctor or nutritionist.

DAIRY-FREE FOODS

Recipes and ingredients will vary between different manufacturers, so it is impossible to give a definitive safe list, but there are certain generic food categories that do not contain dairy products. These include:

- Fruit (fresh, canned, frozen).
- Fruit juices (fresh, frozen, canned, bottled and UHT).
- Fish (fresh, frozen without batter, crumb coating or sauce, canned).
- Meat, poultry, game, bacon, offal and Quorn (not processed products).
- Pasta (fresh and dried), rice and other grains.
- Beans and pulses (dried and canned)
- Nuts and seeds.
- Vegetables (fresh, frozen, dried).

In addition, the following items can generally be eaten safely, but always check the labels:

BAKING INGREDIENTS
- Flour, cornflour, arrowroot.
- High quality dark chocolate.

- Mincemeat.
- Marzipan, ready-to-roll icing.
- Desiccated and creamed coconut.
- Dried fruit, glacé cherries, candied peel, canned fruit pie fillings.
- Ready-to-use pastry is safe if made with pure vegetable fat.
- Filo (brush with oil, not butter).

BEVERAGES
- Fresh fruit juices and soft drinks.
- Beef, yeast or vegetable extract drinks.
- Most types of drinking chocolate powder and cocoa powder.

BISCUITS
- Grissini (breadsticks), cream crackers, water biscuits.
- Oatcakes, crispbreads, rice cakes, melba toast and matzos are usually dairy-free.

BREADS AND BAKED GOODS
- Bagels, pitta breads and muffins are usually dairy-free.
- Some ready-made pizza bases are dairy-free.

CAKES AND PASTRIES
- Meringues.
- Some fruit pies are dairy-free.

CEREALS
- Most breakfast cereals, such as Cornflakes, Shreddies and Weetabix are dairy-free.
- Porridge oats and some brands of muesli.
- Couscous, bulgur wheat, semolina.

CONFECTIONERY AND SNACK FOODS
- Sweets such as mints, jellies, pastilles and marshmallows are dairy-free, as well as some brands of plain chocolate and, carob.
- All kinds of nuts, tortilla chips, taco shells, pretzels, poppadums, prawn crackers and some crisps.

DAIRY MILK SUBSTITUTES
- Soya milk drinks.
- Nut milks, rice drinks.
- Goat's or sheep's milk (if tolerated).
- Lactose-reduced milk (if tolerated).

Above: Many baking ingredients are dairy-free. Clockwise from top left, yellow and white marzipan, plain dark cooking chocolate, canned fruit pie filling, desiccated coconut, glacé cherries and cornflour are all safe to include.

Above: Some people with dairy or lactose intolerance can tolerate goat's milk, sheep's milk and lactose-reduced milk.

DELI FOODS
- Cooked, sliced meats.
- Some ready-made salads, such as mixed bean salad, Waldorf salad, carrot and nut salad.
- Florida salad, potato salad, coleslaw in mayonnaise, but check that yogurt has not been used as a substitute for the mayonnaise.

DESSERTS
- Jellies.
- Custard powder (not the instant type).
- Sorbets and pure fruit ice lollies.
- Soya desserts and soya yogurts.
- Goat's and sheep's milk yogurts (these are not lactose-free, however, so eat them with caution).

DIPS
- Taramasalata, hummus and fresh tomato or fruit salsas.

FATS AND OILS
- Pure solid vegetable oil, soya spread/ margarine, kosher margarine, lard, beef and vegetable suet.
- Corn, sunflower, safflower, olive, soya, rapeseed and nut oils.
- Mayonnaise, salad cream, Thousand Island dressing (without yogurt) and French dressing.

FISH AND FISH PRODUCTS
- Canned fish or shellfish.
- Smoked fish.

MEAT PRODUCTS
- Most sausages and burgers are dairy-free, but check ingredients.

MISCELLANEOUS
- Bouillon cubes.
- Gravy powders and granules.
- Herbs and spices.
- Olives.
- Onion bhajis.
- Pakoras.
- Samosas.
- Stuffings and breadcrumbs.
- Vegetable spring rolls.
- Vinegar.

Above: Many ready-made deli salsas and salads are dairy-free – and perfect to eat with pitta bread. Try taramasalata, tomato salsa, carrot and nut salad and coleslaw.

Right: Finding the right dairy-free snack shouldn't be too troublesome – you can safely eat tortilla chips, poppadums, some crisps, prawn crackers and taco shells.

SAUCES AND CONDIMENTS
- Relishes, chutneys, pickles.
- Soy sauce.
- Mustard.
- Tomato ketchup, tomato purée, sun-dried tomato paste.
- Most tomato-based pasta sauces.

SOUPS
- French onion, spring vegetable, oxtail, lentil, consommé and minestrone should be safe but many creamed varieties include dairy products.

SOYA PRODUCTS
- Soya mince/chunks.
- Tofu (soya beancurd).
- Soya cheese/spreads.

SWEET AND SAVOURY SPREADS
- Jams and marmalades, honey.
- Peanut butter.
- Sandwich spreads and pastes (check ingredients label).

VEGETARIAN PRODUCTS
- Most burgers, rissoles and sausages are dairy-free, as are all vegan products.

Some "ready meals" (chilled and frozen) are dairy-free. Check the label on individual packages.

FOODS TO AVOID ON A DAIRY-FREE DIET

As well as all the familiar dairy foods, many dairy products and derivatives are used in a wide range of processed foods. Depending on how strict your dairy-free diet needs to be, it may be necessary to avoid all of these foods or just some of them. Check labels if unsure of the ingredients, as there will be variation between products and brands, and take advice from a dietician.

COMMON DAIRY FOODS
- Milk (skimmed, semi-skimmed, whole and powdered).
- Evaporated and condensed milk.
- Cream.
- Crème fraîche.
- Fromage frais.
- Quark.
- Butter.
- Buttermilk.
- Cheese.
- Yogurt.

PROCESSED FOODS THAT MAY CONTAIN DAIRY INGREDIENTS

Beverages and Drinks
- Coffee whitener.
- Malted milk drinks.
- Instant hot chocolate drinks (powdered drinking chocolate and cocoa are usually dairy-free).
- Milkshakes.

BISCUITS
- Most sweet types and some flavoured savoury varieties (for instance, those that are flavoured with cheese).
- Some cereal bars (check label).

Bread and Baked Goods
- Many contain dairy products (check ingredients on individual items).

Breakfast Cereals
- Some muesli-type and some oaty cereals list skimmed milk powder among their ingredients.

Right: There are many processed foods that may contain dairy products, from fairly obvious cream cakes, milk chocolates and cream toffees to less easy-to-spot muesli, savoury biscuits and other baked goods.

Cakes
- Many contain dairy products.

Confectionery
- Milk and some plain chocolate.
- Fudge.
- Toffee.

Desserts
- Custards (ready-made canned, fresh chilled and instant custard mix).

- Ready-made dairy-type desserts and mousses (whether fresh, chilled or frozen).
- Cheesecakes.
- Ice cream (dairy and non-dairy – usually made from skimmed milk and vegetable fat).
- Pancakes and batter mixes.
- Canned rice puddings and other dairy puddings.
- Pudding mixes.

Left: Dairy ice cream and milk chocolate are two dairy foods that unfortunately have to be avoided. Even non-dairy ice cream may have skimmed milk powder or other dairy products added, so always be sure to check the ingredients label.

- Frankfurters and some sausages.
- Some sausage rolls, pies and pastries.
- Pizzas (some pizza bases are dairy-free to use with your own topping).
- Some savoury pie fillings.
- Creamy sauces.
- Many fresh, canned and dried soups.
- Quiches and flans.
- Dips based on yogurt, fromage frais or cheese.

Fats and Spreads
- Dairy spreads.
- Margarine (most brands contain some buttermilk, skimmed milk or whey powder).
- Low or reduced-fat spreads (may contain buttermilk).

Savoury Foods
- Some breadcrumb- and batter-coated items.
- Yorkshire puddings.
- Some "ready meals" (fresh, chilled and frozen).

Sweet Preserves and Spreads
- Chocolate spread/chocolate and hazelnut spread.
- Luxury lemon curd.

Vegetables, Canned or Packaged
- Creamed corn.
- Creamed mushrooms.
- Instant mashed potato.
- Spaghetti (canned in tomato sauce).

WATCHPOINTS

- This list can only serve as a guide as products, particularly processed products, may vary. If one brand is off limits because it contains dairy foods, check all similar products; another brand may be dairy-free. It is also important to check items bought from pharmacies: some sweeteners, medicines and vitamin tablets/capsules may contain dairy ingredients, such as lactose.
- If your doctor has prescribed medication for asthma or eczema, such as inhalers, emollients or steroid creams, you should keep using them at the same time as following your diet.

Below left: Dairy spreads, most margarines, some brands of lemon curd, and chocolate spread all contain dairy products.

Below right: Avoid canned and packaged vegetables, such as creamed sweetcorn and mushrooms, canned spaghetti in tomato sauce and instant mashed potato – they all contain dairy products.

MILK AND DAIRY SUBSTITUTES

There's no need to miss out on choice or taste on a dairy-free diet. A wide range of alternative products is available in supermarkets, health-food shops and wholefood stores as well as from specialist mail-order companies. These substitutes can be used to replace regular cow's milk in hot and cold drinks, on breakfast cereals and for all your favourite recipes. If you can tolerate goat's or sheep's milk, these are also available from large supermarkets and health-food shops, or you may well find a local farm or farm shop with supplies of milk, yogurt and cheese. Milks and creams can be frozen successfully for 2–3 months, which is a real bonus if your supplier lives some distance away.

ALTERNATIVES TO COW'S MILK

Goat's and Sheep's Milk

Both goat's and sheep's milk are just as versatile as cow's milk. Goat's milk has a stronger, tangier taste than cow's milk. Sheep's milk has a higher fat content so is thicker and tastes richer and creamier. It is also slightly sweet, so it is ideal for use in milk puddings. Some individuals who have an intolerance to cow's milk find that they react quite well to these alternatives, but it must be stressed that both goat's milk and sheep's milk can provoke an allergic reaction. Their protein content is similar, although not the same as cow's milk. Neither is lactose-free, so they may well be unsuitable for anyone with more than a mild intolerance. The only way to find out if they are acceptable is to try them and see. (They are not recommended for infants under one year of age.)

Goat's cream is available from some larger supermarkets and health food shops. It has a smooth, sweet taste and can be used as a pouring cream, or whipped and used in desserts and as a topping or filling for cakes.

Soya Milks/Drinks

These drinks are made from soya beans and are widely available, fresh chilled and in UHT cartons, in unsweetened and sweetened versions and as flavoured varieties. They are often fortified with calcium, as soya milk is naturally low in calcium compared with cow's milk, and may also have added vitamins. Soya drinks are lactose-free, low in fat (also some fat-free and full-fat versions are available) and free of cholesterol and may therefore offer positive health benefits. In countries where soya foods are eaten regularly there appears to be less risk of developing certain cancers. The incidence of coronary heart disease and menopausal symptoms also appears to be reduced.

Plain soya milk can be used as a complete milk replacement in both hot and cold beverages, as well as for adding to all kinds of recipes. The flavoured varieties, such as vanilla and chocolate, make an appetizing "milky" drink to replace conventional milkshakes.

However, some allergic individuals may react to the soya protein and – as with goat's and sheep's milk – soya milk is not recommended for infants under the age of 12 months. Where a baby reacts to regular formula milks, dieticians generally advise changing to a special non-allergenic modified formula milk.

Soya cream is a non-dairy alternative to single cream and is widely available in long-life cartons from health-food shops and the larger supermarkets.

Left: Alternative milk drinks include (clockwise from top left) sheep's milk, lactose-reduced milk, soya milk, goat's milk, soya cream, oat drink and rice drink.

Oat Drink

This is a Swedish product made with whole oats, rapeseed oil and pure spring water. It is low in fat and calories, contains no cholesterol and offers another alternative for those on a dairy-free diet. UHT cartons are available from health food shops.

Rice Drink

Another long-life drink, this is made from filtered water, organic rice syrup, sunflower oil, sea salt and vanilla flavouring. It is lactose-free and low in fat and is suitable for vegans or those with a milk allergy or intolerance.

FORMS OF COW'S MILK THAT MAY BE TOLERATED

Lactose-reduced Milk

This is a long-life, full-cream product. Although it is made from cow's milk, its lactose content has been reduced through the addition of a natural lactase enzyme, similar to that normally found in the digestive system.

Heat-treated Milks

Certain milk proteins are affected by heat treatment, which alters their composition and makes them tolerable for older children and adults. You may therefore find that sterilized, UHT and evaporated milk are acceptable if an intolerance is caused by protein rather than lactose.

YOGURTS AND DESSERTS

Yogurt is a fermented milk product, which may contain bacteria with enzymes that can digest the lactose present in the milk to produce lactic acid. It is therefore low in lactose, so even yogurt derived from cow's milk may be acceptable for people with relatively mild lactose intolerance. If cow's milk doesn't suit you but you can tolerate goat's or sheep's milk, you'll find a ready supply of these yogurts. There is also a good range of soya desserts, yogurts and ice cream.

CHEESES

Hard cheeses such as Cheddar, Stilton and Parmesan are relatively low in lactose so small amounts may be safe to eat without causing symptoms.

Alternatively, vegan cheeses, made from soya protein, are available from wholefood or health food shops. There are several types, including variations on Cheddar, Gouda, Stilton, Edam, Parmesan and mozzarella. These cheeses can be used in sandwiches or in cooking, although they may not melt in exactly the same way as similar dairy cheeses.

There's also a good selection of goat's and sheep's cheeses available. Goat's cheeses include Chabichou, Chevrotin, Crottin de Chavignol, Chèvre and Chèvre Roulé, Capricorn and Mendip.

Sheep's (ewe's) milk cheeses include Roquefort and pecorino, and also feta and haloumi. These cheeses are traditionally made from sheep's milk but some brands may be made from or contain some cow's milk, so, as with all food products, it is important to check the label.

Above: The huge range of dairy-free soya products available include (clockwise from top left) soya yogurt, soya dessert, soya milk, marinated tofu (soya beancurd), smoked tofu, hard cheeses, which are similar to Cheddar, Edam and mozzarella, cream cheese and (centre) silken tofu.

FATS AND SPREADS

Choose from dairy-free soya spreads, vegetarian or kosher margarines or pure vegetable fats and oils. These can all be used for spreading, baking, sauces and stir-frying. Check labels on vegetable margarines as they often contain some whey or buttermilk, which is added to bring out the flavour, but is obviously unacceptable to anyone on a dairy-free diet.

TOFU (SOYA BEANCURD)

This is a high-protein, low-fat food made from soya beans. It comes in a block with a firm or soft (silken) texture and is available plain, marinated or smoked. Tofu in all its forms is very versatile and can be used in a wide variety of ways as a basis for both sweet and savoury dishes.

NUTS

Despite nut allergy having been recognized as a real clinical problem, there is still a great deal that is not known about the causes, prevalence and management of this potentially serious disorder. It is not clear why, but the number of people with reported nut allergy seems to be increasing.

A nut, in general terms, is an edible, hard-shelled seed or edible kernel. This definition includes those foods that we traditionally think of as nuts, such as peanuts and hazelnuts, as well as some seeds, such as sesame seeds. Nuts can be broken down into two categories:

Edible tree nuts, which include almonds, Brazil nuts, cashews, hazelnuts, macadamia nuts, pecans, pine nuts, pistachios and walnuts.

Other nuts, which include peanuts, also known as groundnuts or monkey nuts, develop in a seed pod about 10cm/4in below ground level; coconuts (in strict botanical terms the coconut palm is not a tree, but a plant closely related to bamboo and grasses); sesame seeds; and sunflower seeds.

These distinctions are important, because where there is a known allergy to one tree nut, for example, it is advisable to avoid all tree nuts. Similarly, some people with a peanut allergy also report allergy to tree nuts.

NUT ALLERGIES

Individuals who suffer from nut allergy are usually allergic to one of the proteins found in nuts. As with most allergies, the symptoms can vary in type and degree of seriousness, but peanuts are often cited as the culprits because they are the nuts that are usually associated with the life-threatening anaphylactic response.

HOW COMMON ARE NUT ALLERGIES?

It is very difficult to assess the true prevalence, but a limited number of studies have been carried out in the United Kingdom. For example, the incidence of sensitivity to peanuts in four-year-olds in a recent study on the Isle of Wight, was 1.4 per cent. Children as young as one, or even less, have started showing sensitivity, probably because they are being introduced to nut-containing foods early in the weaning diet. In America, it has been suggested that peanuts are second only to milk and eggs in terms of allergy prevalence. Although they are no more allergenic than other tree nuts, peanuts are eaten in larger quantities in the United States than in Europe at present. Peanuts, however, are a cheap source of protein, and are therefore being increasingly incorporated into processed foods in the European market.

SYMPTOMS

These can occur after exposure of the allergen to the mouth or skin, or after ingestion or inhalation. Less serious, although unpleasant, symptoms include: bowel discomfort, a worsening of eczema, nausea, colicky pain and diarrhoea. A rash (urticaria) can develop on the skin within a few minutes of exposure.

Below: There are many different types of nuts and all can be the cause of an allergic reaction.

More serious immediate reactions can be life threatening. These include the swelling of the mouth, tongue and back of the throat, which can make breathing difficult. It is possible to get complete obstruction of the airways. Anaphylactic shock is characterized by a drop in blood pressure, followed by unconsciousness, and, if not treated immediately, death. It can start with a burning sensation in the mouth and throat, and general urticaria. Usually these symptoms can be treated by an immediate adrenaline injection. It is essential, therefore, for people with a known severe sensitivity to nuts to carry emergency adrenaline treatment.

Severe reactions are often associated with people who have a history of asthma, and it is quite common for individuals to have other allergies as well. Unlike other allergies, nut or sesame allergy is generally permanent.

DIAGNOSIS

It is easier to identify the allergen if the reaction is immediate than if there is a delayed reaction. Skin prick tests, in which solutions of the test allergens are applied to the skin, can be used to confirm the diagnosis. These tests are only useful if the reaction involves immunoglobulin E (IgE) antibodies, and are less helpful if there is a delayed response.

Blood levels of IgE can also be measured against a particular antigen using the RAST (Radio Allergo Sorbent Test). This may be more appropriate as it reduces the risk of anaphylactic shock.

MANAGING YOUR DIET

Nuts and nut oils are widely used in the manufacture of cakes, biscuits, confectionery, marzipan, pastries, desserts, breakfast cereals, nut butters and vegetarian dishes. Many ethnic dishes, such as those from China, Thailand and Indonesia, may contain nuts. Sesame seeds are found in many foods, such as hummus, halva, burger buns and sesame oil.

Above: Cakes, ice cream and biscuits often contain nuts and nut oils.

Crude oils may contain traces of protein which can cause a reaction, but refined nut oils (i.e. those which have been neutralized, bleached and deodorized) contain no protein traces, and are considered non-allergenic. Oils to watch are "gourmet" oils which can be blended with crude peanut oil to give them a peanut flavour.

Avoiding the nut(s) that cause problems may be easier said than done because of the widespread use of nuts in manufactured foods. People with a nut allergy have to be very vigilant when reading ingredient labels.

Manufacturers are becoming more diligent in identifying potential allergens in their products. There are specific food safety procedures which manufacturers can put in place to assess the potential risk of contamination of products with nuts, even when they are not an ingredient in the particular food. This assessment forms the basis of the decision whether to include a nut warning on products. It is very unlikely that manufacturers will have a list of their products that are "nut-free", because it is virtually impossible to prove that this is the case, since cross-contamination from other products can occur. The current guidelines recommended for nut labelling are:

• If a food product contains nuts or a nut ingredient, it must be included in the ingredients list.
• If there is a risk of contamination (for example, from a nut-containing product made on the same production line), a nut warning should be given near to the ingredients list.
• Where there is very low risk of contamination (e.g. a product is made on a site which does not handle nuts), no labelling is needed.

If in any doubt about the nut status of a product, it is best to check first with the manufacturer. People with nut allergy should always inform schools, relatives and friends who may be preparing food for them of their condition. It is also advisable to wear a pendant or MedicAlert identification bracelet stating your food sensitivity in case of an emergency.

FISH AND SHELLFISH

Fish is reported to be one of the most common causes of food allergy in adults. In Scandinavia, where fish is part of the staple diet, fish is the most common cause of food allergies. The most likely culprit is a protein, which is believed to be found in many species of fish.

HOW COMMON IS FISH ALLERGY/INTOLERANCE?
Allergic reactions to shellfish in particular are reportedly common in adults. Shellfish include shrimp, lobster, crawfish and molluscs (clams, oysters, mussels and scallops).

SYMPTOMS
These can vary in severity, depending on how sensitive the individual is. In more severe cases, the reaction may be an immediate one, involving the immunoglobulin E (IgE) antibodies. In such cases, urgent medical attention is required. Other symptoms might include sickness, diarrhoea, abdominal cramps, wheezing rhinitis and urticaria. Simply handling fish can trigger a reaction in a sensitive person.

DIAGNOSIS
Unlike pinpointing an allergy to eggs and milk, identifying a fish intolerance or allergy should not be too difficult, because you are more likely to know

when you have eaten fish or shellfish. Eliminate the suspected fish from the diet, and, if symptoms clear up, then the fish can be identified as the culprit.

To confirm diagnosis, a skin test or RAST (Radio Allergo Sorbent Test) is often used.

MANAGING YOUR DIET
As fish and shellfish are not normally "hidden" ingredients in foods, it should be relatively straightforward to avoid fish. Nevertheless, there are still some foods that are derived from fish. Remember that Worcestershire sauce usually contains anchovies, and avoid eating Caesar salad, caviar and roe.

There are different kinds of allergy, however: some people who are sensitive to shellfish may be able to tolerate other types of fish, and vice versa.

Above: A sensitivity to shellfish is not uncommon and crabs, lobsters and prawns are among the most frequent culprits.

Left: Fish allergy is reported to be one of the most common food allergies in adults.

EGGS

It is the white, which makes up about 57 per cent of an egg, that can cause an allergic response in those with a sensitivity to eggs. Albumen, the protein in egg white, is made up of around 40 different proteins. It is some of these that have been identified as allergenic.

HOW COMMON IS EGG INTOLERANCE?

As with all types of food intolerance, it is difficult to give a good estimate of prevalence. It is likely, however, that the incidence is highest in infants under one year, and most have outgrown their sensitivity by the age of two.

SYMPTOMS

The most common reaction is an immediate one (i.e. involving IgE antibodies), occurring within minutes of exposure to egg. Symptoms tend to consist of a rash around the mouth, followed by swelling of the mouth and urticaria (skin rash) on the face. As with severe nut allergy, swelling of the mouth and tongue can occur within minutes, and in severe cases result in anaphylaxis.

In less severe cases, symptoms may not appear until one hour after eating the egg, and might include asthma or a worsening of eczema.

DIAGNOSIS

The diagnosis of egg intolerance relies mainly on medical history. The most reliable way to confirm a suspected egg intolerance is to carry out what is known as a double blind placebo controlled food challenge. In this, neither the person with the suspected allergy nor the observer knows which of the foods being offered contain the test material. Other tests, such as skin prick or RAST, are unreliable for confirming egg intolerance.

MANAGING YOUR DIET

All foods containing egg white, egg yolk, or eggs from hen, turkey, duck, goose or other birds should be avoided by those with an egg allergy. As with nuts, egg is extensively used in a wide range of manufactured foods, such as

cakes, bread, confectionery, custard, mayonnaise, sauces, soufflés, batter mixes and some chocolate products.

Anyone following an egg-free diet should visit a dietician to ensure that their diet is providing them with the right balance of nutrients. The dietician will be able to offer them individually tailored nutritional advice as well as providing some up-to-date information about egg-free products and supplying a "free from" list.

Above and right: Eggs are a common ingredient and are included in many manufactured foods, such as lemon curd, mayonnaise and pasta.

SOYA AND OTHER PROBLEM FOODS

Sensitivity to nuts and milk are well known, but there are a number of other foods that can cause an allergic reaction in sensitive individuals.

These foods include soya beans, cheese, chocolate, coffee, citrus fruits and alcohol, and allergic reactions to them can vary in severity.

SOYA

Hypersensitivity to soya beans is much less common than it is to nuts, for example, but, because soya beans are a major component in processed foods, it is much more difficult to avoid them. It is quite common to have an intolerance to soya beans in addition to a sensitivity to cow's milk.

SYMPTOMS

Some sensitive people will experience an allergic response to soya, although an anaphylactic reaction is rare. As with other food intolerances, the symptoms will vary in severity and type.

DIAGNOSIS

A skin test or RAST (Radio Allergo Sorbent Test) can be useful, but, as with many other allergies, the most reliable way to confirm a soya intolerance is to carry out a double blind placebo controlled food challenge (see Eggs).

MANAGING YOUR DIET

Soya beans and soya bean products are found in many processed foods, such as infant milk formulas, cereals, baked goods, canned tuna, soups and sauces. The allergenic protein in soya bean oils is removed during processing, so refined soya oil is considered safe for those with a sensitivity. Soya lecithin, an emulsifier in many processed foods, is also considered safe, unless symptoms of soya sensitivity continue, in which case it should also be avoided.

Ingredients on food labels which indicate the presence of soya protein:
- soya flour
- soya protein isolate
- tofu (soya beancurd)
- soya protein
- textured vegetable protein
- soy sauce
- miso

Other ingredients to look out for are: vegetable starch, vegetable gum and vegetable broth, as these may contain soya protein.

OTHER PROBLEM FOODS

Cheese, chocolate, coffee and citrus fruits can trigger migraine in sensitive individuals. Alcohol can also cause problems, especially red wine, sherry and port. These foods (and drinks) contain "vasoactive amines", which dilate the blood vessels and can provoke migraines. If you are affected in this way, try to avoid the above foods to see if your symptoms improve.

It's also worth remembering that drinking plenty of water to prevent dehydration and eating regularly (low blood sugar can precipitate a bad headache) can help to prevent recurring headaches.

Above: Cheese, chocolate or red wine can trigger a migraine in sensitive individuals.

Left: Soya beans and products such as tofu (soya beancurd) cause an allergic response in some people.

YEAST

Sensitivity to yeast is sometimes blamed for a number of different complaints, such as thrush, stomach bloating, chronic fatigue and rashes. It is not, however, responsible for causing a true food allergy involving the immune system, and in this sense is not considered a major serious allergen.

A yeast-free and sugar-free diet is often recommended for individuals with a sensitivity to yeast. In some recent studies with patients who had chronic urticaria (skin rash) and a suspected yeast sensitivity, over half found that their skin symptoms cleared up when they followed a low-yeast diet.

Individuals following a yeast-free diet should avoid foods that contain any form of yeast, mould or funghi, such as mushrooms, blue cheese or yeast-leavened breads.

Yeasts in the body do not normally cause any harm. However, there may be some triggers, such as diets rich in sugars and yeasts, oral contraceptives, pregnancy and treatment with certain antibiotics, that can cause yeasts to multiply, resulting in "overgrowth".

Above and left: Foods to avoid on a low-yeast diet include cheese and fermented dairy foods, mushrooms, grapes and mould-ripened cheeses.

Non-dietary treatments include various anti-fungal drugs, such as nyastin, evening primrose oil and garlic capsules. Because yeasts feed on sugar, it is also a good idea to cut down on consumption of sugar and sugary foods and drinks.

Foods to avoid on a low-yeast diet include:

- bread, rolls, pizza, buns
- wine, beer, cider
- grapes, raisins
- mould-ripened cheese
- yeast extract
- vinegar, ketchup, pickles
- fermented dairy products, e.g. yogurt and buttermilk
- malted milk drinks
- tofu (soya beancurd)
- soy sauce

FOOD ADDITIVES

Additives, especially artificial ones, are often blamed for being the cause of all manner of allergic reactions and may produce behavioural problems, especially in young children, though this is a highly contentious subject. Additives are certainly thought to be responsible for upsetting a minority of susceptible people, but the number affected may well be considerably less than is sometimes suggested.

Additives may be natural (extracted directly from natural products), nature identical (made to match something found in nature) or artificial, but those that are man-made are no more likely to cause adverse reactions than natural additives or, indeed, natural foods. It is important, too, to remember why additives are used in food manufacture. Some are purely cosmetic and are used in response to consumer expectations of colour, flavour and texture, but most fulfil important and necessary functions. Without additives, food would not keep as well, so we would have to shop more frequently; there would be a greater risk of food poisoning and we would not be able to enjoy the wide range of convenience foods that we've grown to expect.

WHY ARE ADDITIVES USED?

Additives perform a number of different functions, and they are categorized and grouped according to their function, usually by E number. The E number indicates that the additive has been approved safe by EC regulations. Those listed are the main categories but there are many others, including anti-caking agents, acidity regulators, and so on.

Colours (E100s) These are used to restore colour lost in processing (e.g. canned peas) and to make food look more appetizing. Many are natural colourings, coming from foods such as red peppers, grape skins and beetroot.

Preservatives (E200s) These help keep food safe for longer by preventing the growth of micro-organisms which would cause decay, spoilage and food poisoning. These additives protect our health, reduce wastage and allow us to eat a wider choice of foods all year round.

Antioxidants (E300s) These are used to protect fats and oils in food from turning rancid, changing colour and deteriorating through oxidation. Vitamin E (E306) is used as a natural antioxidant in vegetable oil and ascorbic acid. In fruit drinks vitamin C (E300) prevents the fruit turning brown.

Right: Alcoholic drinks, such as beer, wine and cider, often contain sulphite preservatives and other additives but are not subject to ingredient labelling laws.

Emulsifiers and stabilizers (E400s) Emulsifiers are used to help blend ingredients such as oil and water together and stabilizers are used to prevent them separating again. (These additives are used in soft margarines and salad dressings). Thickeners and gelling agents add smoothness.

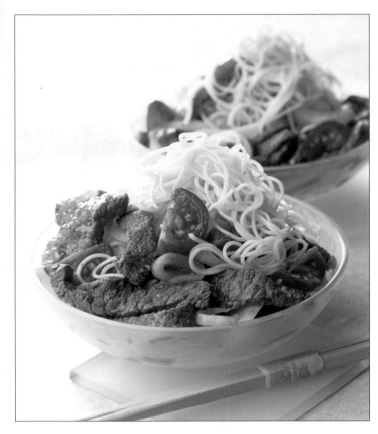

Left: The flavour enhancer MSG (monosodium glutamate) is often added to Chinese restaurant food.

them. The azo dyes, which include tartrazine (E102), a yellow colour used in soft drinks and crumb coatings, may be particularly troublesome. Tartrazine has been linked with hyperactivity in children and also affects asthmatics. Annatto (E160b), which is a natural colour, may also trigger asthma attacks and rashes.

Flavour enhancers MSG is a widely used flavour enhancer, particularly in Chinese dishes. Some people develop allergic reactions, including headaches, nausea, dizziness and palpitations, on eating MSG. These reactions have been given the popular name of "Chinese restaurant syndrome". You may want to check with take-aways and restaurants whether MSG is used and ask for it to be omitted.

HYPERACTIVITY IN CHILDREN

Most children are naturally bounding with energy and can sometimes behave badly. This is all a natural part of growing up and learning social boundaries. It shouldn't be confused with hyperactive behaviour, which can be aggressive, unruly and out of control. It is virtually impossible for the child to settle for long and things become intolerable for the rest of the family. In some cases, artificial colours and preservatives may be implicated but take advice from a dietician before jumping to conclusions.

AVOIDING ADDITIVES

Most supermarkets produce lists of "additive-free" foods. Labels on packs that state stating "no artificial preservatives, colours or flavouring" may also be helpful. Check the labels carefully (all additives must be listed by category and E number or name), and avoid any that you believe cause a reaction. Wherever possible, choose fresh foods.

Flavourings A complex range of natural flavourings and artificial chemical flavourings is added to various foods. As yet these additives do not have any serial numbers.

Flavour enhancers These help bring out the flavour of foods, the most common being MSG (monosodium glutamate/E621). Wherever possible, manufacturers usually prefer to use stocks, herbs and spices for boosting or enhancing flavour.

Artificial sweeteners These are used more and more frequently in place of sugar because they are lower in calories and better for dental health. Saccharin, aspartame and acesulfame-k are the principal artificial intense sweeteners used.

WHICH ADDITIVES MAY BE A PROBLEM?

Preservatives Some asthmatics are sensitive to sulphites (E220–E227), such as sulphur dioxide. Sulphite preservatives are used in beer, wine and cider but, as yet, alcoholic drinks are exempt from ingredient labelling laws. Sodium benzoate (E211), another preservative used in soft drinks, sweets, jam and margarine, can cause problems for asthma or urticaria (skin rash) sufferers and has been linked with hyperactivity in children.

Artificial colours These are recognized as upsetting sensitive people, so many manufacturers, acting in response to consumer demand, have reformulated their products to remove

ALLERGY-FREE SHOPPING

The idea of allergy-free shopping may sound like an impossible task, and it is likely to take more effort than usual. However, once you know what foods or food ingredients you are sensitive to, then you can start to think about how best to adapt your diet to ensure it is nutritionally adequate and well balanced. Try not to worry because there are plenty of sources of help.

PROFESSIONAL ADVICE

If your diet is going to be very restricted – cutting out major food groups, such as dairy products, wheat and eggs, for example – you should ask your doctor to refer you to a professional dietician.

Dieticians have expert knowledge in the field of diet and health, and can offer practical help with planning your daily diet. They will also provide "free from" booklets or lists that will help you to avoid manufactured products containing any problem foods. These booklets and lists include branded products, as well as supermarket own-label brands.

READING LABELS

Whatever food, or foods, you are trying to avoid, the most important task you will have to carry out when shopping is to read food labels. Even if you have "free from" lists from a dietician, supermarket or food manufacturer, it is always wise to check the label, as it is possible that the recipe, and therefore ingredients, will change over time (sometimes this will be indicated by a statement such as "New improved recipe").

By law, food labels must include a list of ingredients, which covers all the ingredients present. Although it will be time consuming to start with, you will soon find that you become good at scanning for the particular ingredients you are looking for.

Below: Even when following a restricted diet, there will still be plenty of different foods that you can eat.

WHAT IF THERE ARE NO FOOD LABELS?

There is no legal requirement to include a list of ingredients on foods that are sold loose (e.g. fruit and vegetables) or unpackaged (e.g. on a delicatessen or bakery counter). If there is any doubt about what ingredients are included in a product, ask the sales assistant or department manager, who will be able to help you. He or she may have a product information guide which will include a breakdown of the ingredients.

ADVICE FROM SUPERMARKETS

All major supermarkets now provide detailed lists of their own-label products that are "free-from" various foods and ingredients which may cause allergies, such as gluten, egg, dairy and soya products.

ADVICE FROM MANUFACTURERS

In addition to supermarkets providing "free from" lists, many food manufacturers also have freephone numbers on packs to encourage consumers to telephone for more information about their products.

Bigger companies will have their own nutrition department and customer care team, who will be able to send you the lists you require and supply any further information you are looking for about particular branded products. Once again, product information lists should have a date on them, so do remember that they will go out of date. It would be impossible to keep these updated constantly in line with any product changes, so always remember to read the label before buying the product.

You may also find now that several companies have started highlighting various allergenic ingredients either in the ingredients list or close to the list. This is particularly true in the case of nut labelling, where there may be a nut warning on the pack. This development has made shopping easier for the nut allergy sufferer.

ALLERGY-FREE COOKING

With the wide range of foods of different nationalities that are available in supermarkets and other specialist shops, it is relatively easy to adapt your diet and soon enjoy a new way of eating. It can be fun and inspiring trying out new foods and products that you might not have chosen before. You will have to experiment with different brands to find ones you like. For example, soya milks tend to vary

Above: It can be fun trying out new products that you have not used before, such as soya milk or tofu (soya beancurd).

considerably in taste, depending on the manufacturer. If you are buying substitute foods such as soya milk, try to buy ones that are fortified with the essential nutrients that you might be missing out on, such as calcium. For tasty, easy-to-prepare dishes, turn to the recipes in the second part of this book. You will find plenty of choice to enable you to meet all your dietary requirements (and to satisfy your tastebuds).

Above: Rice pudding made with dairy-free milk and fruit crumble made with pure vegetable margarine make delicious desserts.

Above: Melon with Parma ham makes a delicious – and safe – starter for most allergy sufferers.

Above: Foods that are coated with breadcrumbs, such as chicken Kiev, should be avoided by those with a wheat allergy.

CHILDREN'S ALLERGIES AND FAMILY MEALS

All children need a healthy diet for growth, energy and physical and emotional development. Evidence suggests that if you encourage healthy food choices at a young age, there's a good chance that these will continue into adulthood and beyond. When a child has an allergy or food intolerance, it's important that he or she is not made to feel different from friends and companions, so try to avoid making a fuss over what the child eats, and wherever possible include as much variety of ordinary everyday foods as is practical and appropriate.

COMMON FOOD INTOLERANCES AND ALLERGIES

The most frequently encountered allergy among infants and young children is to milk, and it usually appears when formula milk or cow's milk is introduced during weaning. The usual symptoms are: asthma, eczema, urticaria (skin rash), or vomiting and diarrhoea. In order to protect against the development of allergies in young children, especially if there is a family history of allergies, breastfeeding is recommended, at least until the baby is four months old, and preferably six months. Most grow out of childhood allergies by the age of five, although those with a family history of allergic illness (known as "atopic") are more likely to develop other allergic conditions and possibly food intolerances in later life. Lactose intolerance may also occur on a temporary basis, as a result of a bout of gastroenteritis. This usually clears up when lactose (milk sugar) is avoided for a short while.

Other common food sensitivities in young children include those to wheat and eggs, usually presenting as asthma or eczema. The medical profession recommends that gluten (found in wheat) should not be introduced into

Below: Dairy products are a common cause of allergic reaction in children.

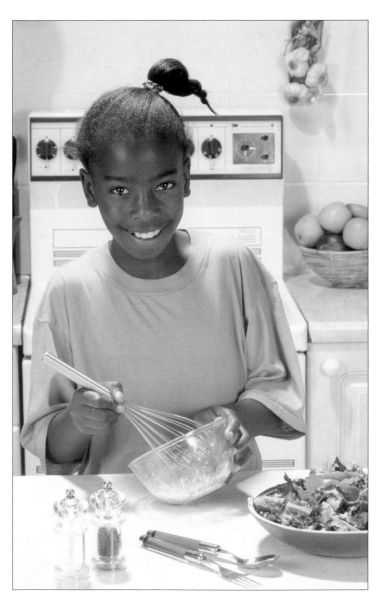

HELPING YOUR CHILD ADAPT

It can be difficult for your child to watch others tuck into jelly and ice cream or chocolate bars if he or she is not able to eat because of a food sensitivity. It is particularly difficult if your child is too young to understand why certain foods aren't allowed. If they are old enough, then explain the reasons why those foods need to be avoided, and focus on all the positive food choices that can be included. Thankfully, there is a much improved selection of alternatives available, such as soya chocolate desserts, which are a delicious choice for children (and adults) on a dairy-free diet.

HEALTHY EATING

The key to a healthy diet containing all the essential nutrients for children's growth and development is balance and variety. It is important to include a range of different foods from the major food groups, in appropriate quantities, every day. Even if you are having to avoid a major food group, such as dairy foods, the diet can still be healthy, as long as suitable alternative foods are included in the diet to make up for lost nutrients. In the case of a diet free from dairy foods, important nutrients that will need to be obtained through other foods include calcium, vitamin A and vitamin B$_2$ (riboflavin).

If you enjoy your food, and make a feature of cooking and preparing it, it is quite likely that your child will also enjoy helping, so that eating and meal occasions are seen as an important and enjoyable part of the day.

Unless your child has a specific sensitivity to them, you do not necessarily have to avoid convenience foods, such as fish fingers, or even to avoid sweets, cakes and other confectionery. These foods can often still be enjoyed as part of a healthy diet, as long as they are eaten in moderation.

Above left: Most children enjoy cooking, so let them help out in the kitchen.

an infant's diet until the age of six months. By this age, it is thought that a baby's intestines are sufficiently developed to cope with gluten, and the risk of coeliac disease is reduced. As far as eggs are concerned, egg yolk can be introduced from around six months, but egg white, which is more allergenic, should not be introduced until babies are nine months old. With babies and young children, it is best to seek advice from your family doctor or health visitor if you are worried about any aspect of your child's health.

Left: Fruit juice, wholemeal toast and cereal can make a healthy breakfast, but may need adapting if you are avoiding dairy products, wheat or citrus fruits.

Below: Spaghetti with meatballs would make a good dairy-free meal for children.

BREAKFAST IDEAS

Breakfast is one of the most important meals of the day; it helps to boost energy levels for the day ahead. Substitute items such as non-dairy milk and gluten- or wheat-free bread, if necessary:

● Breakfast cereals and milk, or a dairy-free alternative, such as soya milk.
● Yogurt and fresh or dried fruit.
● Cooked breakfasts (e.g. poached egg or boiled egg with toast).
● Baked beans on toast.
● Bagels or muffins with a suitable spread and yeast extract or marmalade.
● Grilled mushrooms on toast.
● For a more substantial breakfast, grilled bacon and tomato on toast makes a good choice.
● Include a glass of fruit juice to boost vitamin C levels and to help the absorption of iron from cereals, toast and baked beans.

ADAPTING THE MAIN FAMILY MEAL

Use the recipe ideas in the second part of this book to plan some weekly menus: this will help with shopping, and ensure variety at mealtimes. For healthy eating, base your meals on a starchy carbohydrate food such as pasta, rice and potatoes, and then decide what else to serve with it. Depending on your child's particular food sensitivity, you may have to adapt the recipe slightly (for example, by substituting soya milk or cheese for cow's milk or cheese). Try some of the following ideas:

● Pasta can be served with a wide range of healthy sauces, from tomato to Bolognese.
● Chicken is delicious simply cooked; try chargrilling it and serving with baked potatoes, a barbecue sauce and a mixed salad.

● Fresh or frozen fish, such as cod or salmon steaks and fillets, can be grilled, poached or steamed and served with or without a sauce.
● Lentils are quick to cook and make a delicious vegetarian dish. Cook them with onions, tomatoes and other vegetables.
● If your children aren't keen on cooked vegetables, you could try puréeing them, or using them to make a delicious and wholesome soup.

SUGGESTED PUDDINGS AND DESSERTS

● Fresh fruit.
● Fruit salad.
● Ice cream (this can be dairy-free if appropriate).
● Fruit crumble or pie.
● Baked apples.
● Poached fruit.
● Fruit or milk (use a dairy-free alternative if needed) jelly, set in a small, covered pot.
● Scones, muffins or meringues (gluten-free if necessary).

SCHOOL LUNCHES

When your child goes to playgroup, nursery or school, it is essential that the staff are fully aware of his or her food sensitivities. The easiest option is for you to prepare a packed lunch with items you know your child will eat and enjoy. Just make sure he or she does not swap food items with friends. If you would prefer your child to have cooked school lunches, then talk to the catering staff, who may be quite willing to provide appropriate dishes.

HEALTHY LUNCH BOX IDEAS

- Bread, which can be gluten-free if needed, filled with tuna, ham, cheese (or soya alternative) and salad.
- Some fresh fruit or vegetables (e.g. apple, banana or carrot).
- A yogurt, or soya alternative.
- A drink e.g. carton of apple juice or low-sugar squash.
- A biscuit, plain cake or packet of raisins or other dried fruit.
- For a savoury snack, opt for breadsticks (or gluten-free alternative) or reduced-fat crisps.

ADDITIVES

If you think that food additives (particularly colours and preservatives) are causing an allergic reaction or affecting your child's behaviour, then aim to cut out all "junk" food for a while, and focus on feeding him or her on fresh, simple, homemade dishes. If you would like some professional advice, go along to your family doctor to talk it through.

Top Right: A healthy packed lunch is often the easiest way to ensure that lunch at school is allergy-free.

Right: Additives, such as colourings and preservatives, that are often contained in "junk" food can be responsible for causing an allergic reaction.

ENTERTAINING AT HOME

Eating is one of life's pleasures, and it is even more enjoyable when you are sharing the experience with friends or family, whether formally or informally. When planning the menu, think about your guests and their particular dietary needs. For example, is anyone vegetarian or do they have diabetes? Plan the choice of food around these needs. Think also about the appearance of the food – the colours – as well as contrasting textures and complementary flavours. Will it be a sit-down meal or a buffet-style menu? How filling do you want the meal to be? Is it to be a light supper or a three-course meal?

Catering for special dietary needs doesn't have to mean more work. If you have a dairy intolerance, for example, there are plenty of dishes to choose from in this book that would be suitable for everyone to enjoy, and this saves you having to make something different for yourself. Similarly, if catering for a nut-sensitive friend or someone with a wheat allergy, there are lots of tasty ideas in this book to help you choose a delicious menu.

CHILDREN'S BIRTHDAY PARTIES

When planning a birthday party at home, keep the food as simple as possible. Usually, children are so excited that they do not eat much, but enjoy nibbling on lots of different bite-size snacks. It can be great fun (but hard work) organizing a party at home, and all that's required for younger children are a few party games and lots of time to play and run around.

The key to a successful birthday party is to keep in mind at the planning stage the food intolerances or allergies you will be coping with. Think ahead about what to offer. A choice of sweet and savoury foods is good, but don't put all the sweet foods out at the start or they are likely to be eaten straightaway.

It is easy to decide which foods are appropriate for someone with an allergy and which are not. If a child is nut sensitive, then avoid obvious foods such as peanut butter sandwiches and cakes or biscuits that have nuts such as almonds or hazelnuts in them. The birthday cake may need adapting if a child is allergic to eggs, for example, or to dairy products, gluten or food colouring.

Right: Children with an allergy need not miss out at birthday parties. There are plenty of recipes for birthday cakes that do not contain eggs, gluten or dairy products.

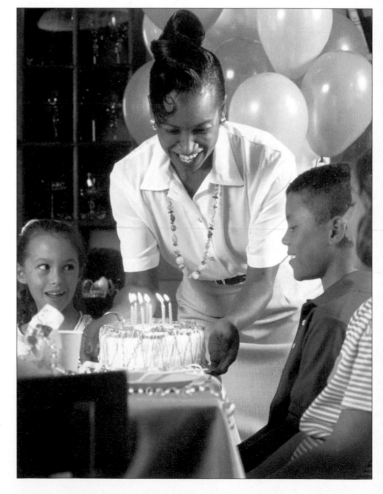

MENU SUGGESTIONS FOR BIRTHDAY TEAS

There are plenty of party foods that are either free from potential allergens or that can be adapted. Listed below are some ideas to help you plan the perfect party.

MENU 1

Savoury snacks
- Small sandwiches, made with ham, tuna, banana, cheese (or soya alternative) and cucumber.
- Chicken drumsticks.
- Plain potato crisps.
- Cherry tomatoes and cucumber sticks.

Sweet snacks
- Chocolate or carob crispie cakes.
- Jelly and ice cream (or non-dairy alternative).
- Fresh strawberries (in season) or seedless grapes.
- Birthday cake.

Drinks: fruit juice or fruit punch, water or squash.

MENU 2

Savoury snacks
- Cheese or tofu (soya beancurd) and pineapple chunks on sticks.
- Grilled bacon and banana rolls.
- Baked potato skins with a variety of dips (make them yourself if you are unsure of the ingredients), such as herb or garlic yogurt (or soya alternative), tomato salsa or hummus.
- Cherry tomatoes and cucumber sticks.

Sweet snacks
- Seedless grapes.
- Chocolate- or carob-dipped strawberries (simply dip in melted chocolate or carob).
- Chocolate or carob marsh-mallows (moisten the tops and place a chocolate or carob button on the top).
- Mini muffins or fairy cakes.
- Birthday cake (can be egg-free or gluten-free if required).

Drinks: fruit juice or fruit punch, water or squash.

meal. To make life easier for everyone, it's important that you let your host know if there are any foods you are unable to eat. Then you can discuss what would be suitable options for the meal. You might like to offer to contribute a dish – a dessert, for example – which will help take the pressure off your host.

When eating out in a restaurant, try to choose one where you know the food is freshly prepared. It is easier for the chefs to cater for your needs if they are making up the dishes themselves, since they may not have all the ingredient details of ready-prepared dishes. It's also a good idea to see the menu in advance if you can, and then to talk to the chef personally about any special requirements.

WHAT TO CHOOSE

If you are in any doubt about what's in a dish, play safe and choose something simple with few ingredients, such as plain grilled or roasted meat, fish or poultry, served with vegetables and potatoes, followed by a fruit-based dessert or an egg-free sorbet.

Above: When eating out, it is often easier to choose a dish, such as roast lamb with haricot beans and salad, that does not rely on a large number of different ingredients.

ADULT GUESTS

Entertaining at home is often a time to try something new, and adults are usually happy to taste new dishes. For a gluten sensitivity, try experimenting with different grains such as buckwheat, to make pancakes, savoury rolls or pastries filled with a vegetable or meat filling; you could also consider a rice dish, chargrilled chicken breasts or fish steak (such as cod, tuna or salmon), as these suit most tastes and are simple to prepare.

At the back of this book, you'll find a delicious selection of mouthwatering recipes to try, most of which are suitable for a number of different food sensitivities and allergies. One example of a menu that would suit most special dietary needs would be a simple vegetable soup, such as Summer Tomato Soup, followed by Chicken Baked with Butter Beans and Garlic, and rounded off with Pears with Ginger and Star Anise. There are lots of different options for delicious yet allergy-free starters, main courses and desserts, so approach the situation as an opportunity to expand your repertoire.

EATING OUT

Lunch and Dinner Invitations

Having a food sensitivity does not mean that you can't eat out anymore, nor does it mean you can't enjoy an evening out in a favourite restaurant. It does mean, however, that you need to do a bit of forward planning, particularly if you are going to a friend's or work colleague's house for a

Left: Many foods that people eat every day contain foods that can cause an allergic reaction. Eggs, nuts, dairy products, wheat and nuts are often contained in cakes, quiches and sauces.

enriching or glazing a dish. It is better to be safe than sorry, so always check if you are at all unsure.

• For people with wheat sensitivity, avoid thick stews, casseroles and soups which may have been thickened using wheat flour.

• Pastries, cakes and desserts may contain dairy ingredients, so if you have a cow's milk intolerance, check first, or choose plain desserts such as fruit salad or sorbet. They are also likely to be made with wheat flour, so should be avoided by those with wheat sensitivity.

• Some Indian and Chinese dishes, such as tandoori and tikka dishes, sweet and sour pork and spare ribs, can often contain artificial colours and preservatives.

SAFE SEASONINGS

People with a wheat or gluten sensitivity should avoid seasoning food with ground white pepper – sometimes flour is added to make the pepper last longer. Stick to ground black pepper instead.

FOODS TO AVOID

Depending on the type of food or foods that you are sensitive to, there are a number of foods you might need to avoid in a restaurant. Here are some general guidelines.

• If you are nut sensitive, avoid foods containing nuts and seeds (e.g. cakes, marzipan, some breads, biscuits and cheesecakes). Refined nut oils (e.g. sesame oil) should not cause problems, but if in doubt, choose something that you know does not contain any potential problem foods.

• For people with egg intolerance, watch out for "hidden" eggs, which are often used for binding, thickening,

ALLERGY-FREE MENU SELECTIONS

Below are some safe menu selections which would be suitable for most types of food intolerances as they exclude most of the main food allergens.

STARTERS

• Melon.
• Grapefruit.
• Mixed fruit cocktail.
• Melon with Parma ham.
• Clear soup (e.g. vegetable soup without thickening).

MAIN COURSES

• Plain grilled, roast or fried meat, fish or poultry.
• Simple fish dishes (e.g. poached or steamed fish).
• Rice dishes.
• Vegetable stir-fries.

DESSERTS

• Fresh fruit salad.
• Fruit sorbet (can be egg-free).
• Stewed fruit or dried fruit.
• Pavlova (suitable for wheat-sensitive people but not for people with egg allergy).

WHICH CUISINE IS BEST?

Each cuisine has its own hallmarks, and, depending on your food sensitivity, you will probably find one that suits your tastes and dietary requirements. Here are a few pointers.

• Italian: famous for pasta and pizzas, Italian food is probably least suited for someone with a wheat sensitivity (although you might find some tasty risotto dishes on the menu). You can usually also find fresh fish and plenty of salads on an Italian menu.

• Indian: a variety of different meat and vegetable curries is on offer, so there is usually something to suit most people. Watch out for cream, ghee (clarified butter) and yogurt if you are following a dairy-free diet.

• Chinese: mainly rice and noodle based, with fish, vegetables and some meat. Very little dairy produce is used.

• French: tend to be rich dishes, relying heavily on dairy ingredients, especially cream, butter and cheese.

PICNIC FOOD

There is something very special about eating outdoors. Picnics can be informal snacks or more extravagant affairs which take more thought and time to prepare. Whatever the occasion, it's a good idea to prepare some food in advance. For an informal family picnic, choose a selection of cold meats and fresh crusty bread, with tomatoes, celery and cucumber. Fresh fruit makes an easy dessert.

For a special picnic, try some of the following: chicken drumsticks or wings; slices of pizza; sticks of raw vegetables, such as cucumber, carrot, peppers, celery and mangetouts; cherry tomatoes; a quiche or flan (wheat- or egg-free if appropriate); and a variety of salads, such as pasta or rice salad, a leafy salad or a bean salad. For dessert, take some baked goods, made without problem foods (e.g. an egg- or gluten-free cake with a jam filling or gingerbread), as well as plenty of fresh fruit.

Below: Picnics are great fun for a family day out but, as with meals at home, a little thought as to your choice of food will help to make them a great success.

HEALTHY EATING
FOR DIABETICS

Over the last few years, the recommended diet for people with diabetes

has changed substantially. A diabetic diet need not be all about denial

but should focus, instead, on eating healthy, well-balanced meals –

high in fruit, vegetables and fibre and low in fat, salt and sugar.

This chapter contains all the information you will need,

from diagnosis to management.

INTRODUCTION

By the time you pick up this book you (or someone close to you, such as a friend, child or parent) may already have been diagnosed as diabetic, so you may have a pretty good idea of what being diabetic is and what it involves. However, since understanding a situation is often the key to coping with it, it may be worth reviewing what you actually know.

Don't be intimidated by the wealth of rather technical information in the next few pages. The principles of dealing with diabetes are really very simple and soon become easier to cope with.

Most diabetics, especially those who have been diagnosed recently, lead normal lives, and some go on to excel in sports, which many non-diabetics could only dream of. So, take heart – and read on.

WHAT IS DIABETES?

The name, *diabetes mellitus*, comes from two Greek words (*diabetes* – a siphon; *mellitus* – honey, because the urine of a diabetic tastes sweet) and describes a condition in which the sugar (or glucose) circulating in the blood cannot be absorbed properly. This results in abnormally high blood glucose levels, which can cause both short- and long-term problems.

To explain in a bit more detail: Glucose (a form of sugar) is the body's main fuel – it provides us with our energy. We absorb glucose from starchy and sugary carbohydrate foods, such as potatoes, rice and beans, breads, biscuits, cakes, sugar and sweets. As we chew, enzymes in saliva start breaking down these foods, a process that is continued by the acids in the stomach. As the food progresses on into the gut, digestive juices from the pancreas and gall bladder get to work, and by the time the food reaches the bowel it has been broken down into simple particles (including glucose), which are absorbed through the bowel wall into the bloodstream. The glucose in the bloodstream moves on through the liver where much of it is stored for future use, and into body cells where it is either burned up to provide energy or stored for future use.

However, the glucose in the blood cannot enter the cells in the liver or any other part of the body unless a chemical (insulin) effectively "opens the door" into those cells. Insulin is a hormone that is manufactured in the pancreas (the glandular organ that lies

behind the stomach but in front of the backbone) and stored there until rising glucose levels in the bloodstream set off a chemical reaction, which releases the insulin. Once in the bloodstream, the insulin links into the body's cells through what are called insulin receptors (a procedure which is rather like two space ships docking). This linkage precipitates chemical changes in the cell walls, which allow the glucose through into the cell where it can be converted into energy.

In a non-diabetic this monitoring and replenishment process happens automatically so that the body's cells are continually fed with sufficient glucose for their energy needs, while excess glucose is stored in the cells. In a diabetic the system fails either because the pancreas does not produce any insulin at all (Insulin Dependent Diabetes Mellitus or IDDM) or because the pancreas' supply of insulin is reduced, the supply of insulin receptors is reduced or neither functions very efficiently (Non Insulin Dependent Diabetes or NIDDM).

Despite years of research no one has discovered why it is that the pancreas should (as in the onset of IDDM) suddenly cease to produce insulin, although it would appear that some people have a genetic predisposition to diabetes. In susceptible individuals, a viral disease can act on the immune system to make it turn upon the "beta" cells in the pancreas, which manufacture the insulin, and destroy them. In NIDDM there seems also to be a radical predisposition: the NIDDM

Above: Children and young adults are more likely to be insulin dependent diabetics than non insulin dependent diabetics.

condition is four times more common in Asian communities than in the rest of the population of Britain, for example. However, with NIDDM, which occurs mainly in older and frequently in overweight people (IDDM usually occurs in thin children and people under 30), there does appear to be a link with obesity. Other possible contributory causes to NIDDM in later years could be pancreatic damage through surgery or alcohol abuse; glucose intolerance during pregnancy, which may disappear after the baby is born but leaves a predisposition to diabetes during later pregnancies or in later life; long-term use of some steroids, which raise the amount of glucose in the blood; and overactivity of the thyroid.

DIAGNOSIS AND SYMPTOMS

Diagnosis of insulin dependent diabetes is normally fairly straightforward as the symptoms, although varied, are pretty obvious and can even be quite dramatic. Non insulin dependent diabetes is another matter, since the fall in insulin production may occur over a number of years and the symptoms may be quite slight. Some people with NIDDM have no symptoms at all.

DIAGNOSIS

If you go to a doctor complaining of any of these symptoms (right), he or she will normally check for diabetes.

The first test might be for excess glucose in the urine although, since the glucose levels in the urine tend to fluctuate (and some people have a low threshold so register as having above the normal level without actually being diabetic), the existence of such an excess is not absolute proof of diabetes. It is more usual to be sent for a blood glucose test. This blood will be taken from a vein, not a finger prick. By the time blood reaches the finger through the small blood vessels or capillaries, it has used up some of the glucose it was originally carrying so does not give an accurate picture. So it is important to measure the glucose in blood taken from a vein (the venous plasma glucose concentration). The normal concentration of glucose that you would expect to find, according to World Health Organization (WHO) criteria, is below 7.8 millimols per litre.

A diabetic, according to the WHO criteria, is one whose "venous plasma glucose concentration" when they have been fasting, remains at 7.8mmol/litre, but rises to above 11.1mmol/litre on a random blood sample. Between "normal" and "diabetic" they list a third category of those with "impaired glucose tolerance" (7.8mmol/litre fasting and between 7.8 and 11.1mmol/litre on a random test). These people may return to normal, may go on to develop full-blown diabetes or

remain at the same level. They should, however, follow a diabetic regime and keep themselves as healthy as possible.

TREATMENT

Although serious, even IDDM has become a treatable condition following the arrival of injectable insulin. Provided you are prepared to stick to your regime, there is no reason why you should not lead a full life.

The key to the management and treatment of both IDDM and NIDDM is to take over the job normally performed by the insulin in the body and keep your blood sugar levels normal. Allowing them to get too high, or too low, can cause a variety of problems and is to be avoided. This does not mean getting paranoid about blood sugar levels or diet – merely keeping a sensible watch on both.

For NIDDMs a change in diet, possibly in conjunction with medication to lower blood glucose levels, will frequently achieve the desired result. Indeed, changes to the diet may improve the health of an individual to such an extent that the onset of their diabetes may be viewed as something of a blessing.

IDDMs have benefited from the development of sophisticated blood testing techniques. These usually involve taking a drop of blood from the finger or ear lobe and have made it much easier to control blood glucose levels, either by changing the diet or the insulin dose.

Whether you have been diagnosed as being an insulin dependent diabetic or a diabetic who is non insulin dependent, your doctor will instruct you in the use of your drugs, insulin and glucose testing equipment. He or she will also give you dietary guidance or send you to a dietitian. The principles of a good diabetic diet are described later in this chapter, and the recipe section contains a wide range of suitable dishes.

SYMPTOMS

Thirst (polydipsia) and passing large quantities of urine (polyuria)
If the levels of glucose in the blood are too high, the kidneys no longer filter all the glucose and some escapes into the urine. The extra glucose thickens the urine, it draws extra water with it to help it to flow through the kidneys, and this causes the bladder to fill. The individual needs to urinate often and in copious amounts. At the same time the body becomes dehydrated, which leads to a terrible thirst.

Constipation
As the body becomes more dehydrated, constipation becomes almost inevitable.

Tiredness and weight loss
Since our bodies acquire their energy from glucose, anyone whose body cannot access the glucose circulating in the blood will be short of energy and therefore tired. In an effort to replace this energy, the body will break down other cells/body tissues thus causing a weight loss that can be dramatic.

Blurred vision
Excess sugar in the blood makes it thick and syrupy. In some diabetics, this can upset the focusing of the eyes – their vision becomes blurred.

Infections
When the blood becomes thick and syrupy due to the presence of excess glucose, this may also affect the functioning of the immune system. The undiagnosed diabetic may be prone to all kinds of infections, including skin eruptions, urinary tract infections, such as thrush or cystitis, and chest infections.

Pins and needles
Changes in the blood glucose levels may also affect nerve functions, resulting in tingling or pins and needles in the hands or feet.

ALTERNATIVE THERAPIES

Once the pancreas has given up on insulin production, it can very rarely be "kicked back into action". However, certain alternative or complementary therapies can stimulate pancreatic function, improve the body's insulin response and moderate glucose levels, so they are worth considering both in cases of non insulin dependent diabetes and in the immediate aftermath of the onset of insulin dependent diabetes, when there may still be some residual function in the pancreas.

Equally important is the diabetic's need to keep as fit and healthy – in both mind and body – as possible. It is recognized that stress does more damage to our health than almost anything else – and that many alternative therapies are very helpful in dealing with stress. Yoga, meditation, reflexology, aromatherapy and massage are some of the best-known stress relievers, but many people find spiritual healers, colour therapists or practising T'ai Chi just as helpful.

CHINESE MEDICINE

The Chinese have recognized diabetes as a disease for many thousands of years. However, Chinese medicine approaches the body, bodily functions and bodily malfunctions from an entirely different angle from Western medicine. To a Chinese doctor, diabetes is a sign of disharmony in the body, whose symptoms appear in the upper body (raging thirst, dry mouth, drinking huge quantities), middle body (large appetite and excessive eating accompanied by weight loss and constipation) and lower body (copious urination, progressive weight loss, etc).

Chinese medical treatment would therefore concentrate on restoring the harmony within the individual with the aim of improving the symptoms and addressing the disease.

Even if this approach does not directly affect insulin production or control, improving the body's natural harmony should improve the diabetic's general health and therefore their ability to cope well with diabetes. However, insulin dependent diabetics must not change their insulin regime if they attend a Chinese physician, except on the express instruction of their diabetes specialist.

RELAXATION AND MASSAGE THERAPIES

It is recognized that stress plays a significant role in the development of diabetes. Any therapy that reduces stress and helps you to relax is therefore likely to have a beneficial effect upon control of your diabetes and your general health.

Yoga and meditation have been found to have a positive impact on blood glucose levels, while moderate exercise helps insulin to work more efficiently in the body.

Reflexology helps to tone and relax the body and, although it cannot address the cause of diabetes, it can alleviate some of the side effects.

Left: Yoga and meditation are both said to reduce blood glucose levels by helping you to relax and reduce stress.

SELF MASSAGE

Aromatherapy (massage with essential herbal oils) is not only relaxing, but can also improve circulation and therefore help to heal the leg and foot ulcers to which some diabetics are prone.

The therapeutic potential of aromatherapy oils, although recognized in the past, has been largely ignored until recently. However, it is now realized that concentrated oils (made from the plants and herbs that filled our ancestors' medicine chests) can be very helpful for many specific complaints.

Essential oils are easily absorbed through the skin into the bloodstream and so are particularly effective for circulatory problems. Some oils, such as hyssop, are good for the circulation as a whole; others, such as grapefruit, lemon, lime, fennel and white birch, are lymphatic stimulants; while spike lavender, rosemary, eucalyptus, peppermint and thyme stimulate sluggish circulation. Massage is a good way to apply essential oils as it is relaxing, and it also ensures that the oils are effectively absorbed.

LEG AND FOOT MASSAGE

Self-massage is relatively easy and can help considerably in reducing stiffness and sluggishness of blood flow in the legs.

1 Start a leg massage by working on the thighs, so that any fluid in the calves will have somewhere to go as the upper leg relaxes. Using both hands, knead one thigh at a time, by squeezing firmly between the fingers and thumb.

2 Squeeze with each hand alternately for the best effect, working from the knee to the hip and back. Repeat on the other thigh.

3 Around the knees, do a similar kneading action but just using the fingers for a lighter effect and working in smaller circles.

4 Bend your leg, and if possible raise the foot on to a chair or handy ledge. With your thumbs, work on the back of each calf with a circular, kneading action. Repeat this action a few times on each leg, each time working from the ankle up to the knee.

5 Squeeze the foot with your hands, loosening up the muscles and gently stretching the arch.

6 To complete the massage, use firm pressure with your thumb to stretch the foot. Repeat on the other foot.

FOOD AND HERBAL MEDICINES

Certain foods and herbs, although they cannot reinstate pancreatic function, can help the pancreas to function more efficiently. They may also improve the absorption of insulin and lead to better control of glucose levels in the blood by the body and to improved circulation. This may, in part, be due to the nutrients found in these foods and herbs (see Nutritional Medicine below), but there is increasing evidence that certain foods and herbs have important health-giving properties, which cannot be entirely attributed to their vitamin or mineral content.

FOODS WITH HEALTH-GIVING PROPERTIES

• Whole oats, onions, globe artichokes and pulses all have the ability to reduce blood sugar.
• Wheatgerm, underripe bananas, turkey, fish, walnuts, red peppers and cruciferous vegetables, such as broccoli and cauliflower (all good sources of Vitamin B_6), help to control blood sugar levels.
• Shellfish, lean meat, wholegrain cereals, pulses, pumpkin seeds and nuts are all high in chromium and zinc (diabetics are commonly deficient in both minerals).
• Bilberries have been found to help in the control of diabetic retinopathy.
• Wheatgerm, sunflower seeds, rapeseed oils, almonds and sweet potatoes (all containing high levels of Vitamin E) have been shown to help improve diabetic circulation and neuropathy.
• Fresh nettle juice has been used since Roman times to help stimulate the circulation, while dandelions have an equally lengthy pedigree for the stimulation of the liver (which is where glucose is stored).

Above: Dandelions have been used for years as a stimulant for the liver.

NUTRITIONAL MEDICINE

Effects of nutrient deficiencies
Although it has long been recognized that we need a wide range of vitamins and minerals for our bodies to function efficiently, there is a growing belief that many of today's degenerative illnesses, such as diabetes, could be caused by serious deficiencies in essential micronutrients, such as vitamins, minerals and amino acids. These deficiencies, it is argued, have resulted from our eating overprocessed foods, living in a highly polluted environment and subjecting ourselves to hitherto unknown levels of stress. Research is going on all the time and continues to reveal links between certain degenerative conditions and some particular nutrient deficiencies.

Chromium is an essential trace element. Although it is only present in minute quantities in the body, it appears to be necessary for blood sugar control and the proper action of insulin. Unfortunately chromium is lost from refined carbohydrates during processing. Chromium is difficult to take as a supplement but is absorbed from brewer's yeast, black pepper, calf's liver, wheatgerm, wholemeal bread and cheese.

Vitamins B_6 and B_{12} can both help blood sugar control. Vitamin B_{12} levels can be reduced by certain diabetic drugs, so it is useful to include sources of this vitamin (lean meat and dairy produce) in the diet.

Above: Nutritional supplements can help to ensure that you are getting the right amounts of some vitamins, minerals and essential fatty acids.

Vitamin C is known to strengthen fragile blood capillaries, especially in the eye, and to reduce elevated cholesterol levels – both conditions that affect diabetics.

Zinc, magnesium and potassium are all very important for diabetics, but levels can be seriously depleted through excess urination. Zinc is important for combating infections such as eczema, acne and thrush, many of which afflict diabetics. Magnesium is also important for the proper functioning of the kidneys.

Essential fatty acids There is increasing evidence that a diabetic's absorption of essential fatty acids may be impeded by raised blood sugar or insulin deficiency so taking a supplement, such as Evening Primrose oil, may help prevent diabetic complications.

KEEPING BLOOD GLUCOSE LEVELS NORMAL

The ideal state for a diabetic is for blood sugar levels to remain normal. Careful monitoring of these, a good diet and medication where necessary are basic strategies. However, many other aspects of the diabetic's life may impinge on his or her blood sugar levels.

BLOOD GLUCOSE LEVELS

Changing exercise levels, for example, can affect both the efficiency of insulin uptake and the rate at which the sugar in the blood is used up. Stress of any kind may cause adrenalin release that will increase the level of sugar in the blood. Infections, injuries or operations are seen by the body as stress. The body reacts by releasing adrenalin or other hormones into the bloodstream, and these again push up the sugar levels. Pregnancy causes changes in blood sugar levels, as do monthly periods and the menopause. Medical drugs, especially steroids and some diuretics and anti-depressants, can also affect blood sugar levels. If any of these factors apply, it is essential to monitor your blood sugar levels even more carefully than usual, adapting your diet or adjusting your insulin dose or the levels of the drug you take to lower blood glucose, in consultation with your doctor, if necessary.

Serious fluctuations in glucose levels cause hypoglycaemia (too little sugar) and hyperglycaemia (too much sugar). Both have very specific symptoms, which need to be treated immediately. If dramatic rises (and, more especially, falls) in blood sugar are treated immediately, there are unlikely to be long-term effects. However, persistent slightly raised blood sugar levels of about 8–19mmol/litre do have a number of serious consequences in terms of health.

CORONARY HEART DISEASE

Elevated triglycerides (fats in the blood) are a common feature of poorly controlled diabetes and add greatly to the risk of coronary heart disease (when the arteries supplying blood to the heart "fur up", thus depriving the heart muscle of the blood it needs to function properly), so diabetics need to be particularly careful about eating a low-fat diet and ensuring that they are not overweight.

STROKE

High blood pressure is another area which diabetics need to watch. Keeping their weight normal, stopping smoking and eating a low-fat, low-salt diet will usually help a great deal to minimize the risk of strokes.

Below: Pregnancy will affect blood glucose levels, which need to be monitored.

NEUROPATHY

Diabetic neuropathy is very common in long-term and poorly controlled diabetics. Although there are many variations, neuropathy happens when the nerve ends become damaged (as a result of excess glucose flowing through the capillaries or small veins). Neuropathy normally affects the hands and feet (tingling or pins and needles in the hands and feet is one of the symptoms of diabetes) and can, over a period, result in loss of all feeling in the extremities.

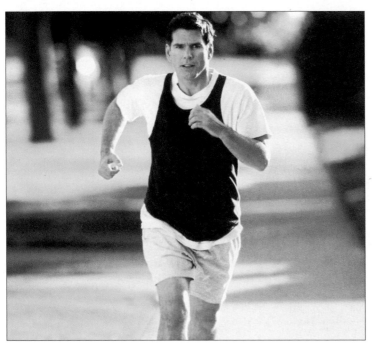

Left: Exercise, such as jogging, increases the rate at which sugar in the blood is used up – to prevent a dangerous dip in your blood glucose level, eat a small carbohydrate snack before, or straight after, any exercise.

Neuropathy presents two problems. One is that the circulation to the more remote areas of the body gets worse and this can lead to infected wounds, bad healing and, in the worst cases, gangrene. Feet and legs are especially prone to damage and need to be looked after and monitored with great care. The other problem is that the feet lose all sensation. This not only affects balance and the ability to walk properly but also means that the sufferer is at risk of injury, perhaps by being scalded by getting into too hot a bath, because their feet have become so insensitive to temperature.

Diabetics can also suffer some damage to their "autonomic nerves". These are the nerves that carry the instructions to the various organs, such as heart, kidneys, bladder and bowels, and tell them what to do. Damage to these autonomic nerves can result in poor bowel or bladder control, failure of the stomach to empty properly and similar problems. Normally all these functions will return to normal when the blood glucose levels are also returned to normal.

KIDNEY AND EYE DAMAGE

The kidneys and the eyes are two areas of the body filled with capillaries or tiny blood vessels that are especially prone to diabetic damage. Excess blood sugar can "clog" up both areas, but whereas kidney damage may be reversed or at least controlled by diet and good blood glucose control, damage to the eyes may be irreversible. Maintaining good control of blood glucose levels will minimize the damage. It is particularly important that diabetics have very regular eye checks and that these should include examination of the retina.

SKIN PROBLEMS

Because raised blood sugar makes one more prone to infection, especially skin infection, badly controlled diabetes will often result in boils, pimples, spots and rashes. Most of these will respond well to good diet and improved control.

This disturbing list of symptoms may sound like a life sentence, but diabetics should remember that most of them only occur when they do not look after themselves. These days, a diabetic diet is almost identical to the healthy diet recommended for all of us – so the diabetic should not be singled out as an oddity.

Because of the huge improvement in both monitoring and injection techniques, even insulin dependent diabetics can check their blood sugar levels and administer their insulin both quickly and discreetly.

However, this does not mean that you should keep your diabetes a secret. For a start, there is no reason to as you can live a perfectly full life with diabetes. Secondly, friends, colleagues and even strangers need to know that you are diabetic in case you should suffer a hyper- or hypoglycaemic attack. This is easily dealt with, but very frightening if you or others do not know what is going on. Consider wearing a diabetic bracelet or tag.

All diabetes does require is that you take it seriously and are organized about dealing with it. You must be rigorous about checking your glucose levels, you must always make sure that you have your insulin or drugs available and you must always ensure that you have extra glucose or carbohydrate food should you need it. Finally, you must be aware that your body is more sensitive to change than that of someone without diabetes so you must pay attention to what it tells you in terms of "feeling different" or unwell. Your body is the best possible monitor of its own condition, so it is important to listen to it.

Hyper- and Hypoglycaemia

Hyper- and hypoglycaemia occur when blood sugar levels rise too high (hyper) or fall too low (hypo).

Hyperglycaemia

The symptoms of hyperglycaemia are usually less dramatic than those of hypoglycaemia, but because tissue damage may result if the blood sugar levels remain too high (usually over 11–12mmol/litre), it is important to get the levels down quickly.

Elevated levels of blood sugar can be the result of uncontrolled long-term diabetes, but there can also be more immediate causes. Forgetting to take your insulin or blood glucose drugs will cause your blood sugar levels to rise, as will eating much more than you usually do – or eating a fattier or more sugary meal than normal.

Reducing the amount of exercise you usually take could affect glucose levels. An infection, illness, operation or accident could all cause blood sugar levels to rise, as can pregnancy and menstruation. Careful monitoring will reveal the raised levels quickly – anything over 11mmol/litre is a bad sign – and changes in insulin, drugs or diet should get you back to normal.

Hypoglycaemia

Hypoglycaemia can occur in non-diabetics whose blood sugar levels fall too low; the official definition is below 2.5mmol/litre. However, this reaction is most frequently seen in diabetics who have taken more insulin than they need or eaten too little – or exercised too much – relative to their last dose of insulin or glucose-lowering drugs.

Although hypoglycaemia symptoms can be dramatic, the results of it are seldom serious, and it is extremely easy to treat. All you need is a rapid intake of sugar in the form of glucose tablets (Dextrose, Dextro), sugar lumps, honey, candy, fruit juice or sweet biscuits. Even when the symptoms are quite extreme, the diabetic will be back to normal in a matter of minutes.

Above: Glucose tablets are a simple and speedy remedy to mild hypoglycaemia.

However, they then need to back up the instant injection of glucose with more solid food, as the excess insulin will quickly absorb the initial blast of glucose and will need something further to work on.

The problem with hypoglycaemia is that the brain is utterly dependent on an adequate supply of glucose to function properly. The first sign that a diabetic is suffering from a "hypo" may be a failure in his or her logical reasoning powers. This can manifest itself as a refusal to accept that they may be suffering from a hypo – which is why it is particularly important for friends and colleagues to know that they are diabetic (and for the diabetic to carry a card or consider wearing an identifying bracelet or badge), so that if their hypo symptoms take the form of denial, someone else can get a glucose tablet into their mouth.

Hypo symptoms vary enormously, but they can often include a lack of concentration, difficulty in making even simple decisions or a feeling of being muddled. A common feeling is that you must finish whatever you are doing, even though you are feeling odd. This is particularly dangerous if you are driving a car, so diabetics must make every effort to recognize and combat this compulsion.

Hypos can often cause behavioural changes and quite violent mood swings. Coordination may also be

impaired. They may stagger as if drunk and have difficulty in performing the simplest task – like unwrapping a glucose tablet!

If unrecognized and untreated, a hypo will eventually cause a diabetic to lose consciousness, but even then an injection of glucagon (the antidote to insulin) will bring the diabetic round to the point where they can be fed a proper dose of glucose.

Since symptoms are so varied, it is important that diabetics are aware of changes in their physical or mental states, that they monitor their blood sugar levels regularly, compensate for any changes in their daily routine and always carry glucose tablets (or the equivalent) with them. Long-term diabetics should be aware that over time symptoms of hypo decrease so that their blood sugar may fall without them having any symptoms at all.

A Few Words of Warning

- Ignore rising blood sugar levels at your peril. Your body's reaction will not be as rapid as with low levels, but if ignored rising blood sugar levels can put you into a coma.
- Never give up your insulin or drug regime – even if you are vomiting. The greater the stress on the body, the greater its need for insulin to combat rising blood sugar levels. Vomiting is serious for a diabetic, so maintain your drug regime and consult a doctor.
- Because the body is infinitely adaptable, some people will feel quite ill when their blood sugar is only slightly raised, while others will still feel relatively okay with seriously high levels. Moreover, long-term undiagnosed diabetics may have got used to having high levels of sugar in their blood so they will not even notice feeling ill.
- It is particularly important to monitor your blood sugar levels on a regular basis, even if you feel fine.

A BALANCED DIET

Diet is the backbone of both insulin dependent and non insulin dependent diabetic management, and the first line of attack in stabilizing blood sugar control. Today, the diabetic diet varies little from the diet that everyone should be eating: to eat at least five portions of fruit and vegetables each day, to take in less than 30 per cent of calories from fat (with most of it coming from mono- and polyunsaturated fats), to reduce the intake of salt (sodium) and sweet foods and to eat plenty of fibre.

THE "OLD" APPROACH

Because sugar is derived from carbohydrates, when the mechanism of carbohydrate absorption was less well understood than it is today, it was thought that diabetics should avoid all carbohydrates. This meant that they had to live on a high-protein, high-fat diet and suffer the side-effects, such as high blood pressure, now associated with such a diet. Moreover, a high-fat diet caused them to gain weight.

Below: Protein is needed for growth and cell repair – wholegrain rice, beans, lentils, tofu (soya beancurd) and walnuts are good sources.

TODAY'S APPROACH

Research into diabetes over the last 25 years has turned a great deal of this thinking on its head, and, although present-day diabetics still have to monitor their diet and their intake of carbohydrate fairly carefully, they are now encouraged to eat plenty of the right kind of carbohydrate foods, and even sugar is sometimes permitted in small amounts.

The food that we eat is made up of proteins, fats, carbohydrates, fibre, micronutrients (vitamins and minerals) and water. The last four (fibre, vitamins, minerals and water) are all essential for the proper functioning of the body but they do not provide us with energy as such (measured in kilo-calories or kilo-joules). This we need to get from proteins, fats and carbohydrates.

PROTEINS

Proteins, which can be found in pulses, peas and beans, soya products such as tofu, nuts, cereals, meat, fish and dairy products such as cheese, milk and cream, are essential for growth in children and for cell repair in adults. We need to get up to 20 per cent of our daily energy intake in the form of proteins.

FATS

Fats (found primarily in meat and dairy products, but also in vegetable and fish oils and nuts) are essential to the proper functioning of the body. However, we need the right kind of fat and the right amount. The average Western diet contains far too much of the "wrong" kind of fat – saturated – which leads to obesity, heart problems and strokes. The recommended maximum number of daily calories that should come from fat is between 30 and 35 per cent. However, unfortunately many Westerners obtain well over 40 per cent of their calories from fat.

Fats are broken down into saturated fats (mainly from the fat on meat, but also dairy products, such as cream, full-fat milk, butter and cheese, and nuts), polyunsaturated fats and mono-unsaturated fats (from vegetable oils such as olive oil and sunflower oil and from fish oils).

The subject of fats is a very complex one, but for the purposes of the diabetic diet the main thing to

Above: Sunflower oil (left) contains mostly polyunsaturated fats, while olive oil is made up of mainly monounsaturated fats.

remember is that saturated fats are to be avoided. These are more likely to cause excess cholesterol to be deposited in the arteries and, because they are higher in calories, obesity is a likely outcome. Diabetics may have high fat concentrations in their blood anyhow (making them more vulnerable to arteriosclerosis), so they should avoid making these levels even higher.

Above: Many different foods, such as (clockwise from top right) milk, pistachio nuts, butter, almonds, cream and cheese, contain fats. Dairy products, such as cheese, butter and milk are all sources of saturated fats, which should be avoided by diabetics, while foods such as nuts are all good sources of polyunsaturated fats, which, along with monounsaturated fats are more beneficial to good health.

CARBOHYDRATES

Carbohydrates (known in "diet-speak" as CHOs) also come in different guises – simple and complex carbohydrates.

Simple (refined or sugary) carbohydrates consist of various forms of what we know broadly as sugar or sucrose. In fact, sucrose is made up from glucose and fructose (fruit sugar). Both are essential for providing us with energy, but glucose is particularly important as the brain depends upon it to function efficiently.

Complex (unrefined) carbohydrates are to be found in starchy foods such as pulses (beans), oats, rice, potatoes and bread. Complex carbohydrates are made up of simple carbohydrates, glucose (see above) and fibres. These fibres may be soluble or insoluble. Soluble fibre is found in pulses, beans and legumes; it breaks down into a sort of gluey solution, which contains the carbohydrate. Insoluble fibre, such as that found in bran and such vegetables as celery and cabbage, has no nutritional value but is used by the body to move food through the system and to push out what is not wanted as waste.

Once they enter the digestive system, complex carbohydrates are broken down by the digestive juices into their components parts – sucrose and fibre. For a diabetic, the virtue of a carbohydrate made up of sucrose and soluble fibre (pulses, peas and beans) is that the gluey solution into which the soluble fibre turns prevents the system from absorbing the glucose too fast, thus giving the diabetic's impaired glucose handling system more time to absorb it. The disadvantage of simple carbohydrates (sugar or sucrose) is that they are absorbed almost immediately into the bloodstream, causing sudden glucose "peaks".

Although studies suggest that if it is eaten along with lots of starchy, high-fibre carbohydrate, a small amount of pure sugar can be successfully absorbed by some diabetics without creating glucose peaks, medical advice would still be to avoid sugar whenever possible. "Sugar" in this context would include sugar itself (in tea or coffee etc), sweets and candies, jams and jellies, cake and biscuits that have been sweetened with sugar or fructose, and sweetened fizzy drinks.

"DIABETIC" FOODS

Medical advice is also to avoid expensive proprietary diabetic foods. Although their actual sucrose content may be lower than that of the foods they are meant to replace, they may use fructose or sorbitol as sweeteners (in fact, there is little medical evidence that fructose is any better for diabetics than glucose, and sorbitol can cause bowel problems if eaten in large quantities). Finally, these foods may make up for their low sugar content by having a high fat content.

Below: Unrefined or complex carbohydrates, which are found in such foods as (clockwise from top right) wholemeal bread, potatoes, oats, haricot beans, rice and lentils, are absorbed more slowly into the bloodstream.

THE DIABETIC'S DAY-TO-DAY DIET

The first thing that the diabetic must remember is that, because the body's ability to absorb sugar is impaired, the system must never be "overloaded". In practice, this means that he or she should have three regularly spaced, moderately sized meals, usually breakfast, lunch and dinner, with two or three regular snacks in between, such as elevenses, mid-afternoon tea and a snack at bed-time. For an insulin dependent diabetic the meals must be timed to come 15–30 minutes after the insulin injection so that the insulin has had time to be absorbed into the bloodstream and is ready to cope with the food.

If you are a newly diagnosed diabetic and have led a rather disorganized life you may find forcing yourself to stick to specific times for meals difficult, but it will prove worth it. And you can console yourself with the thought that if the rest of us ate on a more regular basis we would all feel a lot better too.

BALANCE

A diabetic should try to ensure that each meal or snack is balanced to include carbohydrates, proteins and fats. This is not difficult to achieve, as many snacks naturally contain all three components in varying amounts. A ham sandwich, for example, includes protein (ham), fat (butter, spread) and carbohydrate (bread).

It is important that the diabetic does not miss out on any one element, especially the carbohydrate. Diabetics used to be given a list of what were known as "carbohydrate exchanges", which allocated a carbohydrate value to each food. They then had to work out how much carbohydrate was in each meal they ate, allocate their meal allowance of carbohydrate and devise a "swap" system if they wanted to change any element of this diet. Today, although diabetic practitioners still allot a total carbohydrate allowance to be spread over the day (based on the diabetic's own lifestyle, eating patterns, medication, etc), this does not need to be as rigid as the old exchange system.

AVOIDING EXCESSIVE CALORIE INTAKE

Whereas insulin dependent diabetics are often very thin, non insulin diabetics, especially long-term ones,

tend to obesity – partly of course because the traditional diabetic diet was high in fat and protein. However, it is really important for diabetics to keep their weight down so as to minimize the risk of circulatory and other diseases.

As anyone knows who has tried to diet, the only long-term answer is to reduce the total amount of food that you eat and change the nature of that food.

Reducing the amount of sugar in your diet will set you well on the way; reducing the amount of fat, especially saturated fat, in your diet will help even more. And reduction does not necessarily mean total deprivation.

Right: Fizzy, sweetened drinks, full-sugar jam, sweet biscuits, confectionery, chocolate and cakes aren't completely banned, but consumption of these high-calorie foods should be kept to a minimum.

REDUCING SUGAR

Most diabetic practitioners would prefer their patients to stop sweetening their tea and coffee. However, if the thought is too terrible to contemplate, intense sweeteners, such as Aspartame (NutraSweet, Canderel) or Saccharin (Sweet'n'Low, Hermesetas) are better than sugar, but their consumption should be kept to a minimum.

Sugar in drinks other than coffee and tea – fizzy drinks, colas, etc – should be avoided. Not only do these fizzy drinks give an instant glucose hit (bad for diabetic control), but they are also very calorific (the average cola contains the equivalent of seven teaspoons of sugar). Fizzy water or fresh fruit juice diluted with water are preferred – or, if desperate, the diabetic should try to stick with low-calorie artificially sweetened, fizzy drinks.

Sugar in baking can almost always be replaced with dried or fresh fruits, as is amply illustrated in the recipes that follow. Although fruit contains fructose, this is buried in fibrous flesh, so it is absorbed much more slowly into the system. Fruit also gives a far better flavour to cakes and desserts than granulated sugar, which may be sweet but has no flavour of its own.

Diabetics, indeed all dieters, should also scrutinize labels for added sugar.

Below: Avoid sweetened drinks and opt instead for fizzy water or fresh fruit juice diluted with water.

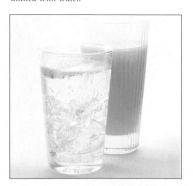

Sometimes this is easy to avoid – buy fruits canned in fruit juice instead of syrup, for example – but it is not always that clear. Remember, too, that on an ingredients list sucrose, fructose, glucose, malt, maltose, honey, lactose and invert corn syrup are all sugar, even though they appear under different names.

Sweets and chocolate bars are to be avoided except as a snack before or after sport. Like the fizzy drinks, these not only deliver an instant glucose "hit", but they are very high in calories. If total deprivation is not to be borne, try buying chocolate, for example, in thin tablets or drops. It is amazing how satisfying even a morsel of chocolate can be if you nibble it rather than wolfing down a whole bar!

If an apple does not fill that sweet gap, try a few raisins or fresh dates.

They are just as sweet as a mint or a bar of chocolate but the sugar they contain is embedded in fibre.

Below: To avoid sugar, choose fruits canned in fruit juice, and try apples, fresh dates and raisins as an alternative snack.

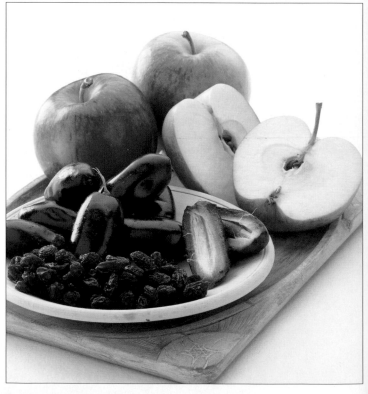

REDUCING FATS

Reducing the amount of calories from fat – especially saturated fat – will help greatly in overall weight control and will also fit in with the specifically diabetic diet. Again, it need not be that difficult to achieve: Some of the new low-fat spreads are really very palatable and work excellently in pastry and baking. Does one always need butter or a spread? A ham sandwich with mustard needs neither; a cheese sandwich tastes as good, if not better, with a little low-fat mayonnaise and a lettuce leaf as it does with a thick layer of butter.

Use extra virgin olive oil or sunflower oil, not butter or lard, for cooking – and try not to use even that. Meat and vegetables for stews do not need to be fried at the start of cooking. If they are cooked long and slowly enough, they will have plenty of flavour. If the occasional plate of chips is a must, use the oven-ready ones, which have a substantially lower fat content. Ideally the chips should be abandoned in favour of a baked potato – but a baked potato filled with canned tuna and sweetcorn, or canned salmon

or baked beans, rather than with piles of butter or cheese!

Like chips, crisps should really be on the forbidden list. Not only are they calorific and high in fat (even the low-fat ones), but they are very salty – and everyone should be reducing their salt intake! Nuts or (even better) seeds, such as sunflower or pumpkin, maybe lightly salted, are just as good with a drink or as a snack and are very much more nutritious.

Above: Choose a low-fat filling for baked potatoes: here the potatoes are simply spiced with curry-flavoured onions and served topped with a generous dollop of low-fat natural yogurt.

USING WHOLEMEAL BREADS AND FLOURS

Even devoted white bread fans, if they persevere with wholemeal breads, will find that although wholemeal breads are not as soft, they have much more flavour. The same applies to using wholemeal flour in baking. The pastry may not be quite as light, but it will be much more flavoursome. There are several other flours that can be used for "lighter but healthier" baking, the most successful of which is gram or chick-pea flour. This is used a lot in Indian cooking. For a diabetic, it has the advantage of being made from a pulse, so it is filled with soluble fibre. Gram flour can be substituted for white flour in most instances and, although the pastry will be a little crumbly, it will taste delicious.

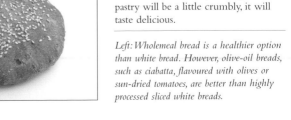

Left: Wholemeal bread is a healthier option than white bread. However, olive-oil breads, such as ciabatta, flavoured with olives or sun-dried tomatoes, are better than highly processed sliced white breads.

FILLING YOURSELF UP

The best way to prevent yourself nibbling – or having the urge to nibble – is by filling yourself up! Try eating large platefuls of colourful salad leaves and raw vegetables, such as tomatoes, peppers, cucumbers, carrots and radishes, or lightly cooked vegetables (most of which, being low in fat and carbohydrate, are on the "eat as much as your like" list for diabetics). For a main meal, bulk out vegetables and salads with cooked wholemeal rice, pasta or cooked beans and pep them up with plenty of chopped fresh herbs and a simple, tasty dressing made from lemon juice and extra virgin olive oil. It is amazing how satisfying they are. Because the food is full of fibre it will take some time for the body to digest, so that feeling of fullness will not have worn off within half an hour as it so often does after over-indulging on sticky cakes.

MONITORING FAT, SODIUM AND FIBRE INTAKES

Diabetics who do not need to lose weight still need to monitor their fat, sodium (salt) and fibre intakes. It is very important that diabetics keep the cholesterol levels in their blood under control to limit the risk of coronary heart disease. They should also keep their blood pressure down. A healthy, low-fat, low-salt, high-fibre diet will do all of these things.

Above: This pilaff of cooked wholemeal rice combined with plenty of lightly cooked vegetables and prawns is a good example of a simple and satisfying yet low-fat meal.

TIPS FOR CUTTING CALORIES

• Using a slightly smaller plate so that a smaller portion still looks generous is an old, but very successful, trick!
• Chewing rather than gulping one's food is another. Some experts recommend up to 20 "chews" per mouthful, but even eight or nine will extend the eating period so that the food seems to go further.
• If the weight still refuses to come off, keep a food diary, in which all food consumed is written down.

• Don't con yourself into thinking that you are sticking to a diet, if you forget about the broken biscuit you ate because it fell out of the packet, the chunk of cheese you ate while grating a piece for a recipe, the half sausage the children had left on their plates or the lick of the jam spoon as it went into the washing up.
• Cutting out these few unnecessary calories may be all that it takes for the required amount of weight to be lost.

MODERATION

It is very easy, especially for a newly diagnosed diabetic, to become obsessed with his or her diet. This is not only unnecessary but is positively unhelpful: all this does is raise stress levels, and it is well recognized that stress is more debilitating for a diabetic than for anyone else.

FOODS TO EAT AND FOODS TO AVOID

It is very important for diabetics to keep to their diet regime the majority of the time, but the occasional "fall from grace" is not likely to be catastrophic, especially if it can be compensated for by extra vigilance at the next meal.

At first it may be hard to remember what is, and is not, allowed, but this will soon become second nature. Comparing calorie values is an easy way to monitor general food intake, but it is even more useful to memorize the key categories of food.

FREE FOODS

These can be eaten whenever and in whatever quantity you want.

- All green and leafy vegetables.
- Cruciferous vegetables (cauliflower, broccoli, turnip, cabbage, etc).
- Salad vegetables (tomatoes, peppers, cucumbers, etc).
- All members of the onion family.
- Green peas and green beans.
- Mushrooms.
- Fruits, such as redcurrants, cranberries and loganberries.
- Tea, coffee, water, tomato juice (in moderation), clear soups.

Left: Eat as much as you like – there's no restriction on the quantity of fresh green beans and peas that diabetics can eat.

Below: Fruits, such as (clockwise from top) pears, grapes, nectarines, raspberries and plums must be counted as part of a diabetic's daily carbohydrate allocation, but make ideal between-meal snacks as well as instant high-fibre desserts.

Above: Salad vegetables, such as fresh tomatoes, cucumbers and a variety of colourful peppers, can be eaten in whatever quantity you want – they are very low in sugar, fat and calories, yet are a good source of micronutrients.

GOOD CARBOHYDRATE/ PROTEIN FOODS

These are good for diabetics to eat, but must be counted as part of an overall carbohydrate and protein allocation.

- All pulses, beans and peas.
- Brown rice and wholemeal pasta.
- Oats, wholemeal flours, breads, unsweetened biscuits, etc.
- All root vegetables.
- All fresh fruits.
- All canned fruits as long as canned in fruit juice, not syrup.
- Dried fruits.
- Unsweetened breakfast cereals that are also high fibre.
- Lean meats or meat products.
- Fresh and frozen fish.
- Low-fat cheese, skimmed milk and low-fat yogurts.
- All soya products.

Right: Soya beans and tofu (soya beancurd) are good foods for diabetics to eat, although soya margarine, a healthy alternative to butter, is still a fat so use it sparingly.

BORDERLINE FOODS

This list reflects carbohydrate foods and fatty foods that are less good – alright to have sometimes in specific quantities but not to be overindulged in.

- White flour, bread, unsweetened. biscuits, pastry, rice and pasta.
- Cornflour, arrowroot, semolina.
- Unsweetened breakfast cereals.
- Any fried potato products, such as chips and crisps.
- Full-fat cheese, cream, full-fat milk and yogurt.
- Fatty meats, including sausages.
- Salty meats and fish products.
- Fruit juices.
- Reduced-sugar jams, marmalade and other spreads.
- Alcohol.

Left: Borderline foods, such as (clockwise from top) full-fat milk, full-fat, sweetened yogurts, full-fat cheeses and cream, can be eaten occasionally, but don't over-indulge.

BAD FOODS

These are to be avoided whenever possible and, when eaten, only to be consumed in very small quantities.

- Sugar: caster, granulated, demerara; also honey and golden syrup.
- Sweets, such as candies, chocolate.
- Full-sugar chewing gum.
- Jams, marmalades and similar spreads that are full-sugar.
- Sweet biscuits, cakes and buns made with white flour and sugar.
- Desserts made with refined flours and refined sugar.

Above: Chocolate biscuits, cakes and buns are best avoided by diabetics.

- Fruit canned in syrup.
- Ice cream and ice lollies.
- Fruit squashes, sweetened drinks (including fizzy drinks and colas).
- Sweetened breakfast cereals.

Below: They are no longer banned entirely, but sweet treats, such as (clockwise from top left) golden syrup, caster sugar, honey, icing sugar and demerara sugar should only be eaten in very small quantities.

ALCOHOL

Alcohol, such as red wine and lager (*right*), is not entirely off limits for diabetics but must be taken in moderation and calculated into the diet. Beware of low alcohol drinks. Because less of the sugar has been converted to alcohol, they may contain more sugar. Conversely, low-sugar drinks may contain more alcohol! Remember, too, that alcohol is calorific; if you are trying to lose weight, keep your consumption low. It is also important to remember that excess alcohol consumption puts a strain on the liver and the pancreas – both organs that are already under pressure in a diabetic.

ABOUT THE RECIPES

We hope that many of the recipes in this collection will give you ideas for other dishes that will fulfil the diabetic diet criteria. Any good cookery book should encourage experimentation, so feel free to adapt any of the recipes.

Our aim has been to include many recipes that diabetics can enjoy. We have tried, therefore, to introduce ingredients, such as pulses and beans, that are high in soluble fibre and low in fats and sugars. Many of the main course dishes add lentils or dried beans to meat or vegetables, and use olive or sunflower oil for cooking. Much of the baking makes use of low-fat spreads and fresh or dried fruit (although you will find the occasional chocolate treat).

Sodium Levels Regular stock cubes can be very high in salt, so look out for "natural" or "organic" stock cubes with no added salt. Whenever possible, buy "no added salt or sugar" canned beans and vegetables, avoid fish canned in brine and go for canned fruit in natural juice rather than in a sugar syrup.

ARTHRITIS PREVENTION

Food has a direct impact on the symptoms of many arthritis sufferers.

Some foods reduce inflammation, and others are rich in the nutrients

essential for the healthy functioning of joints and muscles.

This chapter offers practical advice on managing arthritis, examines

some possible allergy-triggers and explains how to follow

an exclusion diet.

INTRODUCTION

Arthritis is a condition that can affect any of the joints, but is especially prevalent in the load-bearing or particularly hard-working areas, such as the knees, hips, ankles, wrists and hands. In the Western world it is estimated that up to half the population will suffer from an arthritic disorder of the joints at some point in their lives, and that many of these people will be severely troubled by constant pain, stiffness and disability. This is obviously a depressing prospect.

Arthritis cannot be treated as a single disease. There are at least six common forms and up to 100 lesser known types, excluding the rheumatic ailments that are often confused with arthritis. Although it is just as painful as arthritis, rheumatism (including fibrositis/fibromyalgia, bursitis, frozen shoulder and aching neck) is a less serious condition affecting muscles, ligaments and tendons.

Human joints are extremely complex and flexible structures, but they require "good maintenance" for efficient, long-term function. It is when a joint is damaged that arthritis can set in. Damage can be caused by a wide variety of incidents: trauma or accident, abnormal stress, maybe even viral infection or an inflammation. Confusingly, damage may not always lead to arthritis and, as yet, beyond a genetic predisposition, doctors have been unable to identify why some people develop arthritis-related conditions while others do not.

THE STRUCTURE OF A JOINT

A joint is made up of two connecting bones, separated and cushioned by cartilage. Cartilage is water-filled, spongy tissue with no blood vessels and no nerve endings, so cartilage itself never hurts. The joint is held together by a tubular structure attached to the ends of the bones. This is lined with a synovial membrane and lubricated by synovial fluid, which allows the moving parts to rub against each other with minimum friction. The joint is stabilized by muscles, ligaments and tendons on both its inside and outside.

CHANGES IN A DAMAGED AND ARTHRITIC JOINT

The protective cartilage is vital to the proper functioning of the joint. If the cartilage is damaged in any way it is less efficient as the cushion separating the bones.

When the cartilage ceases to perform its cushioning function properly there are several consequences. Initially there appears to be some water loss, after which the cartilage thickens and then softens. Small rips may appear and gradually deepen into tears, which may extend as far as the bone. The bone ends may be damaged or the joint capsule and synovial membrane may become damaged or inflamed. The surrounding tendons and ligaments may also be strained. Eventually, the bone attempts to repair the damage by forming bone spurs, and these stretch the sensitive membrane covering the bone to visibly deform the joints, causing further strain on the surrounding membranes and muscles. The synovial lining, fluid and capsule become inflamed and the joint stiffens.

Although the cartilage has no feeling, the other parts of the joint, including the bone, are very pain sensitive. Increasing pain and stiffness lead to immobility, and experience shows that immobility only makes the condition worse. This explains why most arthritis sufferers find their condition more painful in the morning after lying still all night, than later in the day after moving around.

Left: Osteoarthritis often occurs in the joints that bear the most stress. Keen gardeners may find arthritis particularly painful in their knees, due to long hours of weeding.

Right: Arthritis can affect people of any age, even children. Juvenile arthritis can be particularly distressing, but the good news is that most children outgrow the condition, with no long-term effects.

TYPES OF ARTHRITIS

Although arthritis can take many different forms, the basic joint problem is the same for each type.

OSTEOARTHRITIS

This is the most common form of arthritis, usually associated with increasing age and degeneration. It is also more common in women. Osteoarthritis often occurs in a joint that has been injured or stressed, particularly those joints that do the most work – fingers and thumbs, wrists, knees, hips, ankles and toes. Bony spurs form around the joints and, along with inflammation, make movement difficult and painful.

Progressive joint deterioration can create secondary problems, such as carpal tunnel syndrome, which occurs when arthritis of the wrist causes nerves to be pinched. Not only does this produce pain, but also weakness and loss of control in the hands. Arthritis of the neck can cause severe headaches. Arthritis of the spine can cause radiating pain into the arm or leg (known as sciatica), or injury to the spinal column or to the nerves within the spinal canal.

RHEUMATOID ARTHRITIS

This condition tends to occur in younger people. It is very dramatic and unpredictable and has been known to disappear as suddenly as it appears. It causes inflammation, pain, swelling and joint damage, especially in the hands and wrists, feet, knees and elbows. In severe cases rheumatoid arthritis can affect the internal organs – lungs, heart, liver, kidneys and lymph nodes.

Although no single cause has been found for rheumatoid arthritis, there is evidence to suggest that food allergies,

nutritional deficiencies and viral, parasitic and bacterial infections contribute to the condition.

ANKYLOSING SPONDILITIS

This is an inflammatory condition of the lower back, and it can spread both up and down the spine. It is most common in men.

JUVENILE ARTHRITIS

Symptoms include pain, fever, swelling and skin rash. The condition seems to improve over time, leaving the child with little serious joint damage.

PSORIATIC ARTHRITIS

A condition in which psoriasis (patches of raised, flaky and itching skin) and arthritis are combined.

VIRAL ARTHRITIS

This illness can follow a viral infection, whether or not the person already suffers from arthritis.

LUPUS ERYTHEMATOSUS

This condition causes inflammation of the connective tissue. Symptoms are influenza-like, including aching muscles and joints, fever and fatigue.

GOUT

This is caused by an excess of uric acid in the system. The acid crystals are deposited around joints and tendons, causing inflammation and pain. It can usually be controlled by drugs and by avoiding purines (substances rich in uric acid), which are found in liver, kidneys, shellfish, sardines, anchovies and beer.

TREATING ARTHRITIS

Conventional medicine, on the whole, does not accept a link between food and arthritis. However, there is evidence to suggest that food intolerance and micro-nutrition (essential vitamins, minerals and trace elements) may play a significant role, especially in cases of rheumatoid arthritis.

CONVENTIONAL TREATMENT

Despite the fact that many people are disabled by the various forms of arthritis, medical science can offer no cure. Treatment therefore falls into four areas.

• **Minimizing stress on affected joints** Patients are often advised to lose weight. Although no one is quite sure why, it would appear that being overweight can negatively affect joints, including those that are not weight-bearing (fingers and wrists).

• **Keeping affected joints mobile** Regular, gentle exercise and physiotherapy will keep joints as supple as possible.

• **Reducing the pain of arthritis** Various pain-relieving drugs are used, normally corticosteroids and non-steroidal anti-inflammatory drugs (NSAIDs). Although they may relieve at least some of the inflammation and pain, they do nothing to reverse, or even slow down, the progress of the disease. These drugs can have serious side effects. Even short-term use of steroids can cause weight gain, the one thing that arthritics do not want. Long-term use can cause brittle bone disease or osteoporosis, muscle wasting, skin eruptions and damage, poor wound healing, fluid retention, eye disorders, nutritional deficiencies, even mental disturbance. NSAIDs most frequently cause stomach ulceration.

• **Clearing up infections** Some forms of arthritis (for example, certain cases of rheumatoid arthritis) seem to be set off by bacteria, such as salmonella, campylobacter or yersinai. Joint pains can linger for months or years. In such cases antibiotic treatment may be useful.

ALTERNATIVE TREATMENT

There are occasional cases where dramatic results are achieved by the exclusion or inclusion of one particular food in the diet. However, most people will find that a combined approach, following some of the suggestions below, will result in an improvement in their symptoms, if not a total cure.

• **Dietary manipulation of inflammation** This means eating foods that are most likely to reduce inflammation in the joints.

• **Vitamin and mineral supplementation** Eating a diet rich in the vitamins and minerals needed to minimize the damage caused by arthritis, while taking supplements to counteract possible deficiencies.

• **Exclusion diet** Pinpointing and then removing a particular food, such as wheat or tomatoes, that triggers arthritis or makes the symptoms worse.

• **Weight control** Following a diet to keep body weight down.

OTHER CAUSES

As with most other illnesses, stress seems to make arthritis worse and prevents healing, so minimizing stress is an important part of both complementary and conventional forms of treatment.

There is also some evidence to suggest that, although imbalance in the gut flora (an overgrowth of the yeast *candida albicans*) will not actually cause arthritis, it may well make the symptoms worse.

Left: A doctor will often recommend physiotherapy for joints affected by arthritis, as immobility only aggravates the condition. A gentle massage will help to keep your joints as supple as possible.